经典珍藏版

许渊冲英译
毛泽东诗词

中国出版集团
中译出版社

《毛泽东诗词选》1993 年版

出版者的话

• • •

早在 1993 年，毛泽东主席一百周年诞辰之际，中译出版社（原中国对外翻译出版公司）便出版了许渊冲先生翻译的《毛泽东诗词选》，书中收录了 50 首诗词。这也是先生的英译本在中国大陆首次正式出版。

2015 年，我们根据国内通行的毛泽东诗词版本，增补了 17 首诗词，定名为《许渊冲英译毛泽东诗词》出版。在这本书的编辑过程中，我们发现某些诗词译文版本不一的情况。后来有机会登门请教，许渊冲先生告诉我们，他从上世纪六十年代开始翻译毛泽东诗词，中间不断修改，但是 1993 年的版本是比较可靠的。

此次再版，我们收集了国内和香港出版的多个译本，做了细致的编辑校对工作，存疑之处，与先生共同商定，希望能够奉献给读者一个权威可靠的译本。

先生素有保存历史资料的习惯，他二十世纪七十年代的译文打印稿，此次也将作为别册呈现给读者。这份珍贵的资料忠实再现了先生的翻译过程，“吟安一个字，捻断数茎须”，足见译事不易，译诗不易。

先生将毕生的精力投注在翻译上，并在2014年获颁“北极光”杰出文学翻译奖，在这一领域攀至顶峰。他“择一事，终一生”的精神激励着后辈学人。

谨以此书向许渊冲先生致敬。

原　序

今年是父亲诞生 100 周年纪念。

父亲是革命家，也是诗人。他的诗，非文人墨客的遣兴之作。“诗言志”，父亲诗中的一题、一景、一人、一事，无不记述着中国革命发展的可歌可泣的英雄业绩。古往今来，有“史诗”一说，父亲的诗篇，连贯起来，可谓中国革命的不朽史诗。

父亲是富于感情的人，情感升华为诗，诗就有了生命。大悲大喜，大雅大俗，均寄托了他对人民的情怀。读他的诗，就是理解他这个人。

父亲虽已离我们而去，但他的诗作已成为我们民族的文化瑰宝，成为人类文化史上一颗璀璨的明珠。在今天的世界上，有着巨大的影响。

在父亲诞辰百年之际，中国对外翻译出版公司出版了这个新的译本。我们写下这短短的几句话，作为奉献给父亲的一瓣心香。

是为序。

毛岸青

邵華

一九九三年

The 1993 Edition Preface

• • •

The year 1993 is the centenary of our father's birth.

Father was a poet as well as a revolutionary. However, his poetical writings are unlike those of some men of letters which involve private concerns. As the saying goes, "poetry expresses genuine feelings." There is not one line or one episode in father's poems but portrays some soul-stirring, heroic deeds of the Chinese people in their revolutionary struggles. In the West, there is the word "epic." Father's poetical writings, in their entirety, deserve to be called a spectacular epic of the Chinese revolution.

Father was a man with very rich emotions, which he often crystallized into poems, full of vigor and life. The great sorrows and joys, alive in his poems through expressions magnificent or popular, all bear witness to his profound love for the people. To read his poems is to get to understand him as a man.

Though father has long since left this world, his poetical writing now form a part of the cultural heritage of our nation and even become gems in world literature. Enormous is their impact on the present world.

On the occasion of the centenary of father's birth, China Translation & Publishing Corporation plans to produce a new English version of our father's poems. We pay tribute to his beloved memory by writing a short preface to the new book.

Mao Anqing
Shao Hua
1993

目录

CONTENTS

正 编

1 贺新郎·别友 002

Tune: Congratulations to the Bridegroom
TO YANG KAIHUI

2 沁园春·长沙 006

Tune: Spring in a Pleasure Garden
CHANGSHA

3 菩萨蛮·黄鹤楼 010

Tune: Buddhist Dancers
YELLOW CRANE TOWER

4 西江月·井冈山 014

Tune: The Moon over the West River
MOUNT JINGGANG

5 清平乐·蒋桂战争 018

Tune: Pure Serene Music
THE WARLORDS FIGHT

6 采桑子·重阳 *022*

Tune: Picking Mulberries
THE DOUBLE NINTH

7 如梦令·元旦 *026*

Tune: Like a Dream
NEW YEAR'S DAY

8 减字木兰花·广昌路上 *028*

Tune: Shortened Form of Magnolia
ON THE GUANGCHANG ROAD

9 蝶恋花·从汀州向长沙 *032*

Tune: Butterflies Lingering over Flowers
MARCH FROM TINGZHOU TO CHANGSHA

10 渔家傲·反第一次大"围剿" *036*

Tune: Pride of Fishermen
AGAINST THE FIRST "ENCIRCLEMENT" CAMPAIGN

11 渔家傲·反第二次大"围剿" *040*

Tune: Pride of Fishermen
AGAINST THE SECOND "ENCIRCLEMENT" CAMPAIGN

12 菩萨蛮·大柏地 *044*

Tune: Buddhist Dancers
PLACE OF BIG CYPRESS

13 清平乐·会昌 *048*

Tune: Pure Serene Music
HUICHANG

14 十六字令三首 *052*

THREE POEMS OF SIXTEEN WORDS

15 忆秦娥·娄山关 *058*

Tune: Dream of a Maid of Honor
THE PASS OF MOUNT LOU

16 七律·长征 *062*

THE LONG MARCH

17 念奴娇·昆仑 *066*

Tune: Charm of a Maiden Singer
MOUNT KUNLUN

18 清平乐·六盘山 *071*

Tune: Pure Serene Music
SPIRAL MOUNTAIN

19 沁园春·雪 *073*

Tune: Spring in a Pleasure Garden
SNOW

20 七律·人民解放军占领南京 *078*

CAPTURE OF NANJING BY THE PEOPLE'S
LIBERATION ARMY

21 七律·和柳亚子先生 *082*

REPLY TO MR. LIU YAZI

22 浣溪沙·和柳亚子先生 *088*

Tune: Sand of Silk-Washing Stream
REPLY TO MR. LIU YAZI

23 浪淘沙·北戴河 *092*

Tune: Ripples Sifting Sand
THE SEASIDE—BEIDAIHE

24 水调歌头·游泳 *095*

Tune: Prelude to the Melody of Water
SWIMMING

25 蝶恋花·答李淑一 *100*

Tune: Butterflies Lingering over Flowers
THE IMMORTALS—REPLY TO LI SHUYI

26 七律二首·送瘟神 *104*

GET AWAY, PEST!

27 七律·到韶山 *109*

SHAOSHAN REVISITED

28 七律·登庐山 *111*

UP MOUNT LU

29 七绝·为女民兵题照 *114*
MILITIA WOMEN—INSCRIPTION ON A PHOTO

30 七律·答友人 *116*
REPLY TO A FRIEND

31 七绝·为李进同志题所摄庐山仙人洞照 *120*
THE IMMORTAL'S CAVE—
INSCRIPTION ON A PHOTO TAKEN BY LI JIN

32 七律·和郭沫若同志 *122*
REPLY TO COMRADE GUO MORUO

33 卜算子·咏梅 *127*
Tune: Song of Divination
ODE TO THE MUME BLOSSOM

34 七律·冬云 *131*
WINTER CLOUDS

35 满江红·和郭沫若同志 *133*
Tune: The River All Red
REPLY TO COMRADE GUO MORUO

36 七律·吊罗荣桓同志 *140*
ELEGY ON COMRADE LUO RONGHUAN

37 贺新郎・读史 *142*

Tune: Congratulations to the Bridegroom
READING HISTORY

38 水调歌头・重上井冈山 *146*

Tune: Prelude to the Melody of Water
MOUNT JINGGANG REASCENDED

39 念奴娇・鸟儿问答 *151*

Tune: Charm of a Maiden Singer
DIALOGUE BETWEEN TWO BIRDS

副 编

40 五古・挽易昌陶 *168*

ELEGY ON YI CHANGTAO

41 七古・送纵宇一郎东行 *176*

SEEING LUO ZHANGLONG OFF TO JAPAN

42 虞美人・枕上 *182*

Tune: The Beautiful Lady Yu
WRITTEN ON MY PILLOW

43 西江月・秋收起义 *186*

Tune: The Moon over the West River
THE AUTUMN HARVEST UPRISING

44 六言诗·给彭德怀同志 *188*

GENERAL PENG DEHUAI

45 临江仙·给丁玲同志 *190*

Tune: Immortal at the River
TO DING LING

46 五律·挽戴安澜将军 *194*

ELEGY ON GENERAL DAI ANLAN

47 五律·张冠道中 *196*

AFTER LEAVING YAN'AN

48 五律·喜闻捷报 *200*

REJOICING OVER THE VICTORY

49 浣溪沙·和柳亚子先生 *202*

Tune: Sand of Silk-Washing Stream
REPLY TO MR. LIU YAZI

50 七律·和周世钊同志 *204*

IN REPLY TO COMRADE ZHOU SHIZHAO

51 五律·看山 *206*

MOUNTAIN VIEWS

52 七绝·莫干山 *208*

MOUNT MOGAN

53 七绝·五云山 210
THE RAINBOW CLOUD MOUNTAIN

54 七绝·观潮 212
WATCHING THE TIDAL RISE

55 七绝·刘蕡 214
LIU FEN

56 七绝·屈原 216
QU YUAN

57 七绝二首·纪念鲁迅八十寿辰 218
ON THE 80TH ANNIVERSARY OF LU XUN'S BIRTHDAY

58 杂言诗·八连颂 224
ODE TO THE EIGHTH COMPANY

59 念奴娇·井冈山 230
Tune: Charm of a Maiden Singer
MOUNT JINGGANG

60 七律·洪都 234
NANCHANG, CAPITAL OF JIANGXI

61 七律·有所思 238
YEARNING

62 **七绝·贾谊** *242*
JIA YI

63 **七律·咏贾谊** *244*
ON JIA YI

原译序 *247*

正编

1

1

贺新郎

别友

一九二三年

挥手从兹去。
更那堪凄然相向，
苦情重诉。
眼角眉梢都似恨，
热泪欲零还住。
知误会前番书语。
过眼滔滔云共雾，
算人间知己吾和汝。
人有病，
天知否？

今朝霜重东门路，

照横塘半天残月，

凄清如许。

汽笛一声肠已断，

从此天涯孤旅。

凭割断愁丝恨缕。

要似昆仑崩绝壁，

又恰像台风扫寰宇。

重比翼，

和云翥。

● ● ●

这首词最早发表在一九七八年九月九日《人民日报》。

Tune: Congratulations to the Bridegroom

To Yang Kaihui[1]

1923

Waving my hand, I part from you.
How can I bear to face you sad and drear,
Telling me your sorrow anew?
Keeping back a warm dropping tear,
Your eyes and brows reveal
The bitter grief you feel.
The misunderstanding arose from what I wrote,
But it will melt like clouds that fleet and mists that float.
In the human world, who
Knows me better than you?
Does heaven know
Man's weal and woe?

The road of Eastern Gate with morning frost is white.
The waning moon halfway up the sky sheds her light
So sad and drear
On the Pool Clear.
The whistle shrills and broken is my heart.
From now on, we'll be lonely, far apart.
Of sorrow let's cut off the string,
Of grief let us break through the ring,
Just as Mount Kunlun thrusts its cliffs asunder
Or the typhoon sweeps the world under.
Then like two birds we'll fly
And cleave the clouds on high.

• • •

1 Yang Kaihui (1901–1930) was the wife of Mao Zedong. The poet wrote this poem when he parted with her to carry out revolutionary activities elsewhere. Yang was arrested and put to death by the Kuomintang reactionaries at Changsha in 1930.

2

沁园春

长沙

一九二五年

独立寒秋，
湘江北去，
橘子洲头。
看万山红遍，
层林尽染；
漫江碧透，
百舸争流。
鹰击长空，
鱼翔浅底，
万类霜天竞自由。
怅寥廓，
问苍茫大地，
谁主沉浮？

携来百侣曾游。
忆往昔峥嵘岁月稠。
恰同学少年，
风华正茂；
书生意气，
挥斥方遒。
指点江山，
激扬文字，
粪土当年万户侯。
曾记否，
到中流击水，
浪遏飞舟？

● ● ●

这首词最早发表在《诗刊》一九五七年一月号。

Tune: Spring in a Pleasure Garden

Changsha[1]

1925

Alone stand I in autumn cold,
Of Orange Islet at the head,
Where River Xiang goes north. Behold!
Hills upon hills are all in red,
Woods upon woods in crimson dressed.
The river green down to the bed,
A hundred ships in speed contest.
Far and wide eagles cleave the air;
Up and down fish glide o'er depths clear:
All creatures under frosty skies vie to be freer.
Brooding o'ver immensity there,
I wonder in this world so vast and dim,
Who decides who will sink or swim.

With many friends I oft came here.
How thick with salient days those bygone times appear!
When, students in the flower of our age,
Our spirit bright was at its height,
Full of the scholar's noble rage,
We criticized with all our might.
Pointing to stream and hill,
Writing in blame or praise,
We treat'd like dirt all mighty lords of olden days.
Do you remember still,
Swimming mid-stream, we struck the waves to stay
The boats speeding their way?

• • •

1 Changsha is the capital city of Hunan Province, where Mao Zedong spent his youth, studying and working in the First Normal School from 1914 to 1918, when he liked to swim with his schoolmates in River Xiang around the head of Orange Islet.

3

菩萨蛮

黄鹤楼

一九二七年春

茫茫九派流中国，
沉沉一线穿南北。
烟雨莽苍苍，
龟蛇锁大江。

黄鹤知何去？
剩有游人处。
把酒酹滔滔，
心潮逐浪高！

• • •

这首词最早发表在《诗刊》一九五七年一月号。

Tune: Buddhist Dancers

Yellow Crane Tower[1]

Spring 1927

Wide, wide through the land flow nine streams full to the brim;
Long, long from south to north threads one line deep and dim.
Shrouded in grizzling mist and drizzling rain.
Tortoise and Snake hold the River in chain.

Where is the yellow crane in flight,
Leaving for visitors a site?
I pledge with wine the endless flood;
With rolling waves upsurges my blood.

• • •

1 The Yellow Crane Tower was built in 223 on the Snake Hill in Wuchang, Hubei Province. It was named so as a legend said that an immortal ascending to heaven on the back of a yellow crane had passed the place and may poems had since been written about it. One of the best-known poems reads as follows:

Once an immortal passed on his yellow crane's back;
The deserted Yellow Crane Tower was left there.
The yellow crane was gone and will never come back;
Only eternal white clouds still float in the air.

The tower was famous for the views it commanded over the Yangtze River and its tributaries flowing from the west to the east, over the Beijing-Guangzhou railway extending from the north to the south, over the two hills, one like a tortoise protruding from the northern bank, and the other like a snake uncoiling on the southern bank, both seeming to hold tight the great Yangtze River.

This poem was written in the spring of 1927 when Mao Zedong, after making an investigation on the peasant movement in Hunan Province, came to Wuhan, capital of Hubei Province, to attend a joint meeting of representatives of peasants of various provinces. The right opportunists in the Communist Party dared not support the great revolutionary struggle of the peasants, preferred to desert the peasantry and thus left the working class and the Communist Party isolated and without help. As a result, the Kuomintang murdered leaders of the workers, suppressed peasants and made war on the people in the summer of 1927. Then Mao Zedong left Wuhan to organize the famous Autumn Harvest Uprising in Hunan Province.

4

西江月

井冈山

一九二八年秋

山下旌旗在望，
山头鼓角相闻。
敌军围困万千重，
我自岿然不动。

早已森严壁垒，
更加众志成城。
黄洋界上炮声隆，
报道敌军宵遁。

● ● ●

这首词最早发表在《诗刊》一九五七年一月号。

Tune: The Moon over the West River

Mount Jinggang[1]

Autumn 1928

Flags and banners in sight below,
Drum-beats mingle atop with bugle-blast.
Surrounded ring upon ring by the foe,
Aloft we still stand fast.

Our ranks as firm as rock,
Our wills form a new wall.
O'er Huangyangjie the cannons' roar
Announces the foe's flight at night-fall.

• • •

1 In the autumn of 1927, Mao Zedong, after organizing the famous Autumn Harvest Uprising in Hunan Province, established a revolutionary base in Mount Jinggang in the Hunan-Jiangxi border area. On August 30, 1928, Kuomintang units from Hunan and Jiangxi attacked Mount Jinggang. The defending troops under Mao Zedong, numbering less than one battalion, fought back from their position at Huangyangjie (or Huangyang Block), routed the enemy and saved the base.

5

清平乐

蒋桂战争

一九二九年秋

风云突变，

军阀重开战。

洒向人间都是怨，

一枕黄粱再现。

红旗跃过汀江，
直下龙岩上杭。
收拾金瓯一片，
分田分地真忙。

● ● ●

这首词最早发表在《人民文学》一九六二年五月号。

Tune: Pure Serene Music

The Warlords Fight[1]

Autumn 1929

A sudden burst of wind and rain:
The warlords fight again.
Sowing on earth but grief and pain,
They dream of reigning but in vain.

O'er River Ting our red flags leap;
To Longyan and Shanghang we sweep.
A part of golden globe in hand,
We're busy sharing out the land.

• • •

1 In March 1929 began the war between Chiang Kai-shek and the warlords of Guangxi Province. In August broke out the war between Chiang Kai-shek and two warlords of the Northern clique. Taking advantage of the clash between these warlords, the Red Army led by Mao Zedong crossed the River Ting in the west of Fujian Province, liberated Changting, Longyan and Shanghang in September, established revolutionary bases there and redistributed the land to the peasants.

6

采桑子

重阳

一九二九年十月

人生易老天难老，
岁岁重阳。
今又重阳，
战地黄花分外香。

● ● ●

这首词最早发表在《人民文学》一九六二年五月号。

Tune: Picking Mulberries

The Double Ninth[1]

October 1929

Nature does not grow old as fast as man;
Each year the Double Ninth comes round.
And now the Double Ninth comes round.
How sweet are yellow flowers on the battleground!

• • •

1 On October 11, 1929 (the Double Ninth Festival, that is, the ninth day of the ninth month by the lunar calendar), Mao Zedong wrote this poem on horseback while leading the Red Army to establish revolutionary bases in the west of Fujian Province, after liberating Changting, Longyan and Shanghang.

一年一度秋风劲，
不似春光。
胜似春光，
寥廓江天万里霜。

See autumn reign with heavy winds once every year,
Unlike springtime.
Far more sublime,
The boundless sky and waters blend with endless rime.

7

如梦令

元旦

一九三〇年一月

宁化、清流、归化，
路隘林深苔滑。
今日向何方，
直指武夷山下。
山下山下，
风展红旗如画。

●　●　●

这首词最早发表在《诗刊》一九五七年一月号。

Tune: Like a Dream

New Year's Day[1]

January 1930

Ninghua, Qingliu, Guihua:
Deep forests, slippery moss and narrow paths.
Where are we bound today?
Straight below Mount Wuyi we go our way.
Below,
Below,
The wind unrolls
Red flags like scrolls.

• • •

1 In December 1929 the Red Army held its 9th Party Congress at Shanghang, Fujian Province, then passed by Qingliu, Guihua, Ninghua and marched westward to Mount Wuyi on the lunar New Year's Day, that is, January 30, 1930.

8

减字木兰花

广昌路上

一九三〇年二月

漫天皆白，
雪里行军情更迫。
头上高山，
风卷红旗过大关。

此行何去?
赣江风雪弥漫处。
命令昨颁,
十万工农下吉安。

● ● ●

这首词最早发表在《人民文学》一九六二年五月号。

Tune: Shortened Form of Magnolia

On the Guangchang Road[1]

The sky all white,
The army march in snow, the more eager to fight.
O'erhead loom crags;
We go through the strong pass with wind-frozen red flags.

Where are we hurrying?
Towards the River Gan where snow is flurrying.
Orders out yesterday:
One hundred thousand troops to Ji'an make their way.

• • •

1 In January 1930 the Red Army led by Mao Zedong had crossed the Wuyi Mountains and entered Jiangxi Province. In February it was marching on Guangchang in the southwest of Jiangxi when the poet wrote this poem on horseback. On February 24 the Red Army attacked the Kuomintang troops stationed near Ji'an, an important city on the River Gan in Jiangxi.

9

蝶恋花

从汀州向长沙

一九三〇年七月

六月天兵征腐恶，

万丈长缨要把鲲鹏缚。

赣水那边红一角，

偏师借重黄公略。

百万工农齐踊跃，
席卷江西直捣湘和鄂。
国际悲歌歌一曲，
狂飙为我从天落。

● ● ●

这首词最早发表在《人民文学》一九六二年五月号。

Tune: Butterflies Lingering over Flowers

March from Tingzhou to Changsha[1]

July 1930

Heavenly troops wage war in June on evil lords,
Ready to capture rocs and whales with long, long cords.
Beyond the River Gan a corner blazes red,
Thanks to the army with Huang Gonglue at its head.

A million workers and peasants all leap and bound,
Sweeping Jiangxi, on Hunan and Hubei they pound.
The stirring strains of "the Internationale" rise;
A furious storm comes down for our sake from the skies.

• • •

1 In June 1930 the Third Army Group of the Red Army was ordered to attack Changsha, capital of Hunan Province; the Second to attack Wuhan, capital of Hubei Province; the First under the command of Mao Zedong, to attack Nanchang, capital of Jiangxi Province. When the Third Army Group was in retreat, Mao was ordered to reinforce it, and he wrote this poem on the way from Tingzhou to Changsha. The poet referred to the Red Army as "heavenly troops," to the Kuomingtang troops as "evil lords" with their "rocs and whales," and to the revolution as "a furious storm." Huang Gonglue (1898–1931) was commander of the Third Army fighting along the River Gan, who laid down his life in Donggu, southeast of Ji'an in September 1931.

10

渔家傲

反第一次大“围剿”

一九三一年春

万木霜天红烂漫，
天兵怒气冲霄汉。
雾满龙冈千嶂暗，
齐声唤，
前头捉了张辉瓒。

二十万军重入赣，
风烟滚滚来天半。
唤起工农千百万，
同心干，
不周山下红旗乱。

● ● ●

这首词最早发表在《人民文学》一九六二年五月号。

Tune: Pride of Fisherman

Against the First "Encirclement" Campaign[1]

Spring 1931

Under a frosty sky all woods in gorgeous red,
The wrath of godlike warriors strikes the sky overhead.
Mist shrouds Longgang and dims the thousand peaks
about.
All voices shout:
"Ah! Zhang Huizan is captured by our men ahead!"

Two hundred thousand troops invade Jiangxi again,
Raising a cloud of dust sky-high like hurricane.
Arouse a million workers and serfs to take the gun,
United as one,
How wild below Mount Pillar our red flags will run!

• • •

1 Towards the end of 1930 Chiang Kai-shek employed about 100,000 men, divided into eight columns, with Zhang Huizan as field commander, to attack the Red area in Jiangxi Province, defended by 40,000 men whom the poet described as "godlike warriors." Nine thousand men of the 18th Division under Zhang Huizan occupied Longgang, southeast of Ji'an County. On December 27, 1930 Mao Zedong massed the largest number of troops of the Red Army to attack the headquarters of the 18th Division at Longgang, capturing the entire force of nine thousand men and the divisional commander Zhang Huizan himself, without letting escape a single man or horse. Fearing defeat, the enemy forces retreated in disorder. So ended the first "Encirclement" campaign.

Four months later, Chiang Kai-shek employed again 200,000 men to attack the Red area in Jiangxi Province. This poem was written between the first and the second "Encirclement" campaign. Mount Pillar was a legendary mountain below which furious battles had been fought in ancient times. Here the poet might refer to any battlefield in the Red area, for example, White Cloud Mountain mentioned in the next poem.

11

渔家傲

反第二次大"围剿"

一九三一年夏

白云山头云欲立，
白云山下呼声急，
枯木朽株齐努力。
枪林逼，
飞将军自重霄入。

七百里驱十五日，
赣水苍茫闽山碧，
横扫千军如卷席。
有人泣，
为营步步嗟何及！

● ● ●

这首词最早发表在《人民文学》一九六二年五月号。

Tune: Pride of Fishermen

Against the Second "Encirclement" Campaign[1]

Summer 1931

Atop the White Cloud Mountain the clouds seem to rear;
Below the White Cloud Mountain cry the foes for fear.
Withered trees and rotten wood try hard to come near,
A forest of rifles appear,
But our flying army falls on them from the sphere.

We've marched seven hundred li in days fifteen
From brimming River Gan to Mount Wuyi green.
A thousand foes are swept away as a mat clean.
Someone bewails unseen:
On forts built at each step, alas! he could not lean.

• • •

1 In April 1931 Chiang Kai-shek concentrated 200,000 troops in his second "Encirclement" campaign against the Red area in Jiangxi Province and used the strategy of "consolidating at every step," that is, building a bastion at each step. On April 27 the Red Army led by Mao Zedong, numbering over thirty thousand men, lay in ambush in White Cloud Mountain near Ji'an County. On May 16 two Kuomintang divisions totaling eleven regiments fell into the ambush and lost the first battle. Then from May 16 to 30, the Red Army marched 350 kilometres from the River Gan to Mount Wuyi, fought four battles and smashed the second "Encirclement" campaign.

12

菩萨蛮

大柏地

一九三三年夏

赤橙黄绿青蓝紫，
谁持彩练当空舞？
雨后复斜阳，
关山阵阵苍。

当年鏖战急，
弹洞前村壁。
装点此关山，
今朝更好看。

● ● ●

这首词最早发表在《诗刊》一九五七年一月号。

Tune: Buddhist Dancers

Place of Big Cypress[1]

Summer 1933

Red, orange, yellow, green, blue, indigo, violet, who
Is dancing with a multi-coloured band in the blue?
After the rain the sinking sun is seen;
The mountain pass exhales floods of deep green.

A furious battle raged then on this spot;
The village walls are still riddled with shot.
Dotted today with these traces of war,
The mountain pass looks fairer than before.

• • •

1 On February 9, 1929, the Red Army led by Mao Zedong arrived at the Place of Big Cypress, about ten kilometres to the north of Ruijin, center of the Red area in Jiangxi Province. On February 10, the Red Army beat the 7th Independent Division of Kuomintang which came on its heels to the Place of Big Cypress, and captured over 800 men, including two regiment commanders. Four years later, that is, in the summer of 1933, after winning the battle against the fourth "Encirclement" campaign launched by Kuomintang, Mao Zedong and his Red Army passed again the Place of Big Cypress when he wrote this poem.

13

清平乐

会昌

一九三四年夏

东方欲晓，
莫道君行早。
踏遍青山人未老，
风景这边独好。

会昌城外高峰，
颠连直接东溟。
战士指看南粤，
更加郁郁葱葱。

● ● ●
这首词最早发表在《诗刊》一九五七年一月号。

Tune: Pure Serene Music

Huichang[1]

Summer 1934

Dawn tinges the eastern skies.
Boast not you start before sunrise.
We have trodden green mountains without growing old.
What scenery unique here we behold!

Peaks after peaks outside Huichang, as if in motion,
Undulate until they join with the eastern ocean.
Our warriors, pointing south, see Guangdong loom
In a richer green and a lusher gloom.

• • •

1 In October 1933, Chiang Kai-shek launched his fifth "Encirclement" campaign against the Red area centered on Ruijin in Jiangxi Province. It lasted a whole year, and the Red Army had to withdraw from its base and begin its Long March to the northwest. In July 1934, Mao Zedong came to Huichang, southwest of Ruijin, ascended on the morning of July 23 the high peaks outside the Huichang walls and took a survey of the route to be followed by the Red Army in its Long March.

14

十六字令三首

一九三四年到一九三五年

其一

山，

快马加鞭未下鞍。

惊回首，

离天三尺三。［作者原注］

［作者原注］　湖南民谣：“上有骷髅山，下有八面山，离天三尺三。人过要低头，马过要下鞍。”

其二

山，

倒海翻江卷巨澜。

奔腾急，

万马战犹酣。

其三

山，

刺破青天锷未残。

天欲堕，

赖以拄其间。

● ● ●

这三首词最早发表在《诗刊》一九五七年一月号。

Three Poems of Sixteen Words

1934–1935

I

Peaks!
Whipping the steed without dismounting, I
Look back surprised
To be three-foot-three off the sky.[1]

AUTHOR'S NOTES

1 A folk song runs:

Above there's Mount White Bones;
Below there's Mount Eight Stones.
The sky is three foot three o'erhead.
If you go on foot, bend your head;
If you go on horse, dismount instead.

II

Peaks,
Turbulent sea with monstrous breakers white,
Or galloping steeds
In the heat of the fight.

III

Peaks
Piercing the blue without blunting the blade,
The sky would fall
But for this colonnade.

15

忆秦娥

娄山关

一九三五年二月

西风烈，
长空雁叫霜晨月。
霜晨月，
马蹄声碎，
喇叭声咽。

雄关漫道真如铁，
而今迈步从头越。
从头越，
苍山如海，
残阳如血。

● ● ●

这首词最早发表在《诗刊》一九五七年一月号。

Tune: Dream of a Maid of Honor

The Pass of Mount Lou[1]

February 1935

The wild west wind blows strong;
The morning moon shivers at the wild geese's song.
On frosty morn
Steeds trot with hooves outworn
And bugles blow forlorn.

Fear not the strong pass iron-clad on all sides!
The summit's now surmounted with big strides.
Surmounted with big strides,
Green mountains like the tide;
The sunken sun blood-dyed.

• • •

1 The Pass of Mount Lou was situated to the north of Zunyi County, Guizhou Province, on the communication line between Guizhou and Sichuan. The Red Army on the Long March occupied the Pass twice, before and after the Zunyi Meeting held in January 1935, when Mao Zedong's leadership was established in the Communist Party of China.

16

七律

长征

一九三五年十月

红军不怕远征难，
万水千山只等闲。
五岭逶迤腾细浪，
乌蒙磅礴走泥丸。

金沙水拍云崖暖，
大渡桥横铁索寒。
更喜岷山千里雪，
三军过后尽开颜。

● ● ●

这首诗最早发表在《诗刊》一九五七年一月号。

The Long March[1]

October 1935

Of the trying Long March the Red Army makes light:
Thousands of rivers and mountains are barriers slight.
The five serpentine Ridges outspread like rippling rills;
The pompous Wumeng peaks tower but like mole-hills.

Against warm cloudy cliffs beat waves of Golden Sand;
With cold iron-chain bridge River Dadu is spanned.
Glad to see the Min Range snow-clad for miles and miles,
Our warriors who have crossed it break into broad smiles.

• • •

1 The Central Red Army started from Jiangxi and Fujian provinces on the Long March in October 1934. It advanced westward along the Five Ridges extending over Jiangxi, Guangdong, Hunan and Guangxi provinces. In January 1935 it passed by the twelve peaks of Wumeng Mountain in Yunnan Province. Then it turned to the north, crossed the River of Golden Sand in May and River Dadu spanned by an iron-chain bridge in Sichuan Province. In September it crossed the perpetually snow-capped Min Range and trackless grasslands and finally arrived at the revolutionary base area in northern Shaanxi in October.

17

念奴娇

昆仑

一九三五年十月

横空出世，
莽昆仑，
阅尽人间春色。
飞起玉龙三百万，［作者原注］
搅得周天寒彻。
夏日消溶，
江河横溢，
人或为鱼鳖。
千秋功罪，
谁人曾与评说？

［作者原注］　前人所谓“战罢玉龙三百万，败鳞残甲满天飞”，说的是飞雪。这里借用一句，说的是雪山。夏日登岷山远望，群山飞舞，一片皆白。老百姓说，当年孙行者过此，都是火焰山，就是他借了芭蕉扇扇灭了火，所以变白了。

而今我谓昆仑：
不要这高，
不要这多雪。
安得倚天抽宝剑，
把汝裁为三截？
一截遗欧，
一截赠美，
一截还东国。
太平世界，
环球同此凉热。

这首词最早发表在《诗刊》一九五七年一月号。

Tune: Charm of a Maiden Singer

Mount Kunlun

October 1935

Above the earth, across the blue,
Monster Kunlun in white,
You have feasted your eye on the world's fairest view.
Like three million white jade dragons in flight, [1]
You have chilled the sky through.
When summer melts your snow
And rivers overfow,
For fish and turtles men would become food.
But who has ever judged if you
Have done for ages more ill than good?

Kunlun, I tell you now:
You need not be so high,
Nor need you so much snow.
Could I but lean against the sky
And draw my sword to cut you into three!
I would give to Europe your crest
And to America your breast
And leave in the Orient the rest.
In a peaceful world young and old
Might share alike your warmth and cold!

AUTHOR'S NOTES

An ancient poet said:

> While three million jade dragons were engaged in fight,
> The air was filled with their tattered scales in flight.

Thus he described the flying snow. I have borrowed the image to describe the snow-covered mountains. In summer when one climbs to the top of Min Range, one looks out on a host of mountains, all white, undulating as in a dance. Among the local people a legend was current to the effect that all these mountains were afire until the Monkey King borrowed a palm leaf fan and quenched the flames, so that the mountains turned white.

18

清平乐

六盘山

一九三五年十月

天高云淡，
望断南飞雁。
不到长城非好汉，
屈指行程二万。

六盘山上高峰，
红旗漫卷西风。
今日长缨在手，
何时缚住苍龙？

这首词最早发表在《诗刊》一九五七年一月号。

Tune: Pure Serene Music

Spiral Mountain[1]

October 1935

The sky is high, the clouds are light,
The wild geese flying south are out of sight.
We are not heroes unless we reach the Great Wall;
Counting up, we've done twenty thousand li in all.

Of Spiral Mountain at the crest,
Red flags wave in wanton winds from the west.
With the long cord in hand today,
When shall we bind the Dragon Gray[2]?

• • •

1 The Spiral Mountain whose highest peak is situated to the southwest of Guyuan County, Ningxia, is so called for the way winding up looked like a spiral or six zigzags. It was the last high mountain the Red Army crossed on their Long March.

2 The Dragon Gray refers to the Japanese aggressors.

19

沁园春

雪

一九三六年二月

北国风光，
千里冰封，
万里雪飘。
望长城内外，
惟余莽莽；
大河上下，
顿失滔滔。
山舞银蛇，
原驰蜡象，［作者原注］
欲与天公试比高。
须晴日，
看红装素裹，
分外妖娆。

［作者原注］ 原指高原，即秦晋高原。

江山如此多娇，
引无数英雄竞折腰。
惜秦皇汉武，
略输文采；
唐宗宋祖，
稍逊风骚。
一代天骄，
成吉思汗，
只识弯弓射大雕。
俱往矣，
数风流人物，
还看今朝。

● ● ●

这首词最早发表在《诗刊》一九五七年一月号。

Tune: Spring in a Pleasure Garden

Snow

February 1936

See what the northern countries show:
Hundreds of leagues ice-bound go;
Thousands of leagues flies snow.
Behold! Within and without the Great Wall
The boundless land is clad in white,
And up and down the Yellow River, all
The endless waves are lost to sight.
Mountains like silver serpents dancing,
Highlands like waxy elephants advancing,[1]
All try to match the sky in height.
Wait till the day is fine
And see the fair bask in sparkling sunshine,
What an enchanting sight!

Our motherland so rich in beauty
Has made countless heroes vie to pay her their duty.
But alas! Qin Huang[2] and Han Wu[3]
In culture not well bred,
And Tang Zong[4] and Song Zu[5]
In letters not wide read.
And Genghis Khan[6], proud son of Heaven for a day,
Knew only shooting eagles by bending his bows.
They have all passed away;
Brilliant heroes are those
Whom we will see today!

• • •

1 Author's note: Highlands of Shaanxi and Shanxi.

2 Qin Huang or Qin Shihuang (259–210 BC) was the first emperor of the Qin Dynasty, who had founded a unified empire in 221 BC.

3 Han Wu or Han Wudi (156–87 BC) was the fifth emperor of Han Dynasty, who had resisted foreign aggression.

4 Tang Zong or Tang Taizong (599–649) was the second emperor of the Tang Dynasty, who had made China one of the strongest countries in the world.

5 Song Zu or Song Taizu (927–976) was the first emperor of the Song Dynasty.

6 Genghis Khan (1162–1227) was the first emperor of the Yuan Dynasty, who had made a western expedition as far as Europe.

20

七律

人民解放军占领南京

一九四九年四月

钟山风雨起苍黄，
百万雄师过大江。
虎踞龙盘今胜昔，
天翻地覆慨而慷。

宜将剩勇追穷寇，
不可沽名学霸王。
天若有情天亦老，
人间正道是沧桑。

● ● ●

这首诗最早发表在人民文学出版社一九六三年十二月版《毛主席诗词》。

Capture of Nanjing by the People's Liberation Army[1]

April 1949

Over the Purple Mountain sweeps a storm headlong:
Our troops have crossed the great river, a million strong.
The Tiger girt with Dragon outshines days gone by;
Heaven and earth o'erturned, our spirits ne'er so high!

With our courage unspent pursue the foe o'erthrown!
Do not fish like the Herculean King[2] for renown!
Heaven would have grown old were it moved to emotions;
The world goes on with changes in the fields and oceans.[3]

• • •

1 On April 23, 1949 the People's Liberation Army captured Nanjing, capital of the Kuomintang government, which looks like a crouching tiger girt by a coiling dragon (the Purple Mountain).

2 The Herculean King refers to Xiang Yu, who fought for the throne against Liu Bang, beat him but did not pursue the war to a complete victory, lost one decisive battle and killed himself in 206 BC.

3 Another version:

> Pursue the beaten foe with our courage unspent!
> Don't fish like the Herculean King for renowns!
> Heaven would have grown old if it were sentient;
> The proper way on earth is full of ups and downs.

21

七律

和柳亚子先生

一九四九年四月二十九日

饮茶粤海未能忘，
索句渝州叶正黄。
三十一年还旧国，
落花时节读华章。
牢骚太盛防肠断，
风物长宜放眼量。
莫道昆明池水浅，
观鱼胜过富春江。

● ● ●

这首诗最早发表在《诗刊》一九五七年一月号。

〔附〕　柳亚子原诗

七律·感事呈毛主席

开天辟地君真健，
说项依刘我大难。
夺席谈经非五鹿，
无车弹铗怨冯驩。
头颅早悔平生贱，
肝胆宁忘一寸丹！
安得南征驰捷报，
分湖便是子陵滩。［原注］

［原注］　分湖为吴越间巨浸，元季杨铁崖曾游其地，因以得名。余家世居分湖之北，名大胜村。第宅为倭寇所毁。先德旧畴，思之凄绝！

Reply to Mr. Liu Yazi[1]

April 29, 1949

I cannot forget our tea-drinking at Canton,
Nor our verse exchanged 'neath yellow leaves in Chongqing.
After thirty-one years, back in the ancient town,
I read your fine verse 'mid falling blooms in late spring.
Do not grumble too much for fear your heart should break;
Try to take longer views in judging anything.
Do not complain too shallow is the Kunming Lake.
For watching fish, it's better than River Rich-Spring.

• • •

1 Liu Yazi (1887–1958) was a leftist of the Kuomintang. He became a friend of Mao Zedong in 1925–1926, period of cooperation between the Kuomintang and the Communist Party of China. Sometimes they had tea together in tea-houses at Canton. Fifteen years later Liu Yazi wrote a poem including the following couplet:

In cloudy days the State could not leave us carefree;
The Southern Sea remembers seeing us at sea.

In August 1945 Mao Zedong flew to Chongqing to negotiate with the Kuomintang, Liu Yazi came to the airfield to welcome him, writing another poem including the following couplet:

By your sincerity I know your courage high;
The nation will be glad to see the war gone by.

In Chongqing they had a heart-to-heart talk about which Liu Yazi wrote a third poem including the following couplet:

I have learned more in one heart-to-heart talk with you
Than by ten years' patient diligence I e'er do.

Then Liu Yazi requested Mao Zedong to write a poem in return and Mao showed him "Snow" written in February 1936 (See P71). On March 25, 1949 after the liberation of Beijing, Mao came back to the ancient capital he had left 31 years before, and invited Liu to come back from Hong Kong. On March 28 Liu wrote the following poem:

My Thoughts Presented to Chairman Mao

You excel in making an epoch and new age;
'T was hard for me to turn a warrior to a sage.
I am not a time-serving scholar in debate;
When not warmly received, I will not stay and wait.
In my mind I regret to have my life misspent;
In my heart of my truthfulness I ne'er repent.
Oh! If from the South comes the victory report,
My familiar lake will be my hermit resort.

The "warrior" in line 2 referred to Chiang Kai-shek who refused to negotiate peace with the Communist Party of China. On reading this fine verse, Chairman Mao wrote a poem in reply on April 29, advising him to take part in political activities and spend his rest-days by the side of the Kunming Lake in the Summer Palace of Beijing, instead of going back to retire in his native town in South China (not yet liberated then) as did the famous hermit Yan Guang who fished on the River Rich-Spring in the Eastern Han Dynasty (the 1st century).

22

浣溪沙

和柳亚子先生

一九五〇年十月

一九五〇年国庆观剧，柳亚子先生即席赋《浣溪沙》，因步其韵奉和。

长夜难明赤县天，
百年魔怪舞翩跹，
人民五亿不团圆。

一唱雄鸡天下白，
万方乐奏有于阗，
诗人兴会更无前。

● ● ●

这首词最早发表在《诗刊》一九五七年一月号。

〔附〕柳亚子原词

浣溪沙

十月三日之夕于怀仁堂观西南各民族文工团、新疆文工团、吉林省延边文工团、内蒙古文工团联合演出歌舞晚会，毛主席命填是阕，用纪大团结之盛况云尔！

火树银花不夜天。
弟兄姊妹舞蹁跹。
歌声唱彻月儿圆。［原注］

不是一人能领导，
那容百族共骈阗？
良宵盛会喜空前！

［原注］　新疆哈萨克族民间歌舞有《圆月》一歌云。

Tune: Sand of Silk-Washing Stream

Reply to Mr. Liu Yazi

October 1950

At a song and dance performance during the National Day celebrations of 1950, Mr. Liu Yazi wrote an impromptu poem[1] to the tune of "Sand of Silk-Washing Stream," to which I replied, using the same rhyme sequence.

Dawn came late to Crimson Land[2] drowned in long, long night:
Demons and monsters[3] danced for ages in great delight;
Five hundred million people yearned to reunite.

At the cock's clarion call the world sees broad daylight:
Music plays far and near, songs from Yutian[4] come here,
Our poet's verse attains an unprecedented height.

• • •

1 Liu Yazi's poem reads as follows:

Fiery trees and silver flowers illuminate the night,
Brothers and sisters dance merry to music bright,
Singing the song of "The Full Moon" in great delight.

Without the leadership of one man ever right,
How could the hundred nationalities unite?
The festival attains an unprecedented height.

2 Crimson Land refers to China which had only five hundred million people then.

3 Demons and monsters refer to foreign aggressors and feudal rulers and warlords in China.

4 Yutian is a county in the southwest of the Xinjiang Uygur Autonomous Region.

23

浪淘沙

北戴河

一九五四年夏

大雨落幽燕，
白浪滔天，
秦皇岛外打鱼船。
一片汪洋都不见，
知向谁边？

往事越千年，
魏武挥鞭，
东临碣石有遗篇。
萧瑟秋风今又是，
换了人间。

• • •

这首词最早发表在《诗刊》一九五七年一月号。

Tune: Ripples Sifting Sand

The Seaside—Beidaihe[1]

Summer 1954

On northern land a heavy rain is pouring,
Sky-high white waves are roaring.
Off Emperor's Isle the fishing boats outgoing
All lost to sight in the wide, wide sea foaming,
Who knows where they are roaming?

Over a thousand years ago by the seaside,
Whipping his steed, Wu of Wei[2] took a ride.
Verses on his eastern trip to Mount Stone still remain.
The autumn wind is blowing now as bleak as then,
But changed is the world of men.

• • •

1 Beidaihe is a famous seaside resort not far from Qinhuangdao or Emperor of Qin's Isle, an ice-free port in the northern land.

2 King Wu or the Martial King of Wei (155–220) was one of the three kings who tried to unify the empire in the period of Three Kingdoms. In 207 he came on horse to the Rocky Hill or Mount Stone by the seaside and wrote the following poem:

I came to view the boundless ocean
From Rocky Hill on eastern shore.
Its water rolls in rhythmic motion,
And islands stand amid its roar.
Tree on tree grows from peak to peak;
Grass on grass looks lush far and nigh.
The autumn wind blows drear and bleak;
The monstrous billows surge up high.
The sun by day, the moon by night
Appear to rise up from the deep.
The Milky Way with stars so bright
Sinks down into the sea in sleep.
How happy I feel at this sight!
I croon this poem in delight.

24

水调歌头

游泳

一九五六年六月

才饮长沙水，
又食武昌鱼。
万里长江横渡，
极目楚天舒。
不管风吹浪打，
胜似闲庭信步，
今日得宽余。
子在川上曰：
逝者如斯夫！

风樯动，

龟蛇静，

起宏图。

一桥飞架南北，

天堑变通途。

更立西江石壁，

截断巫山云雨，

高峡出平湖。

神女应无恙，

当惊世界殊。

● ● ●

这首词最早发表在《诗刊》一九五七年一月号。

Tune: Prelude to the Melody of Water

Swimming

June 1956

Having relished a cup of Changsha water
And then a dish
Of Wuchang fish[1],
I swim across the thousand-mile long river,
And as far as can reach the eye,
I find the wide, wide Southern sky.
Braving wild winds and waves, I feel more pleasure
Than strolling in a yard at leisure:
What freedom I enjoy today!
The Master on a stream did say:
"Thus pass all things away!"[2]

Sails in the wind go past,
Tortoise and Snake[3] stand fast;
Great works are on the make:
A bridge will fly from north to south o'er there,
Turning the chasm into a thoroughfare.
Stone walls will stand across the river in the west
To hold back clouds and rains o'er Mount Witch's crest
Until between steep cliffs emerges a placid lake.
Mount Goddess[4] standing still as before
Would be surprised to find no more
The world of yore.

• • •

1 The King of Wu (c. 280) wanted to remove his capital from Jianye (modern Nanjing) to Wuchang, but his people said in opposition:

We'd rather drink a cup of Jianye water
Than eat a dish
Of Wuchang fish.

Here the poet adapted the saying for circumstance.

2 Confucius (551–479 BC) said, "Thus pass all things away night and day."

3 Tortoise and Snake are two hills, one like a tortoise protruding from the nothern bank, and the other like a snake uncoiling on the southern bank of the Yangtze River.

4 A Chinese legend went that Goddess of Mount Witch would come out in the morning in the form of a cloud and in the evening in the form of a shower over Mount Witch, the highest peak along the Yangtze River.

25

蝶恋花

答李淑一

一九五七年五月十一日

我失骄杨君失柳，
杨柳轻飏直上重霄九。
问讯吴刚何所有，
吴刚捧出桂花酒。

寂寞嫦娥舒广袖，
万里长空且为忠魂舞。
忽报人间曾伏虎，
泪飞顿作倾盆雨。

• • •

这首词最早发表在一九五八年一月一日湖南师范学院院刊《湖南师院》。

〔附〕 李淑一原词

菩萨蛮

一九三三年

兰闺索寞翻身早，
夜来触动离愁了。
底事太难堪，
惊侬晓梦残。

征人何处觅？
六载无消息。
醒忆别伊时，
满衫清泪滋。

Tune: Butterflies Lingering over Flowers

The Immortals—Reply to Li Shuyi[1]

May 11, 1957

You've lost your Willow and I've lost my Poplar proud,
Their souls ascend the highest heaven, light as cloud.
The Woodman, asked what he has for wine,
Brings out a nectar of laurels divine.

The lonely Goddess of the Moon, large sleeves outspread,
Dances up endless skies for these immortal dead.
From the earth comes the news of the Tiger o'erthrown.
In a sudden shower their tears fly down.

• • •

1 Li Shuyi was the teacher of Chinese language and literature in the 10th Middle School at Changsha, Willow refers to Liu Zhixun, husband of Li Shuyi and comrade-in-arms of Mao Zedong. He joined the Communist Party of China in 1923 and laid down his life in battle in 1932. Poplar refers to Yang Kaihui, wife of Mao Zedong and intimate friend of Li Shuyi. She was put to death by Kuomintang reactionaries in 1930. In February 1957 Li Shuyi sent to Mao Zedong the following poem written in 1933 in memory of Liu Zhixun, to the tune of "Buddhist Dancers":

I toss about in bed in my lonely room;
My dream of him casts on me a midnight gloom.
This is too much for me to bear,
When I awake to find him not there.

He's gone, but where can he be seen?
I have no news from him for six years.
When I recall the parting scene,
My sleeves are wet with crystal tears.

In reply to this poem, Mao wrote "The Immortals," in which he imagined Yang and Liu had ascended to heaven and were drinking nectar with the woodman in the moon. In answer to Li's question "where can he be seen?" Mao said "Their souls ascend the highest heaven" where lived the Goddess of the Moon. On hearing the news that the Tiger or Chiang Kai-shek was overthrown, the immortals shed tears of joy instead of wetting their sleeves "with crystal tears."

26

七律二首

送瘟神

一九五八年七月一日

读六月三十日《人民日报》，余江县消灭了血吸虫。浮想联翩，夜不能寐。微风拂煦，旭日临窗。遥望南天，欣然命笔。

其一

绿水青山枉自多，
华佗无奈小虫何！
千村薜荔人遗矢，
万户萧疏鬼唱歌。
坐地日行八万里，
巡天遥看一千河。
牛郎欲问瘟神事，
一样悲欢逐逝波。

其二

春风杨柳万千条，
六亿神州尽舜尧。
红雨随心翻作浪，
青山着意化为桥。
天连五岭银锄落，
地动三河铁臂摇。
借问瘟君欲何往，
纸船明烛照天烧。

● ● ●

这两首诗最早发表在一九五八年十月三日《人民日报》。

Get Away, Pest!

July 1, 1958

When I read in *The People's Daily* of June 30, 1958 that schistosomiasis had been wiped out in Yujiang County, thoughts thronged my mind and I could not sleep. In the warm morning breeze next day, as sunlight falls on my window, I look towards the distant southern sky and in my happiness pen the following lines.

I

To what avail were all these streams green and hills blue?
A little germ defied the best physician's skill.
Hundreds of hamlets saw men waste where weeds o'ergrew;
Thousands of dreary homes heard vampires sing their fill.
Riding the earth, one goes eight myriad li a day;
Ranging the sky, one sees Milky Ways from afar.[1]
If the Cowherd[2] inquired about the Plague God, say:
"His joy is washed away just as our sorrows are."

II

The vernal wind awakens myriads of willows;
Six hundred million are masters of wisest sort.
Crimson rain[3], as we wish, turns into fertile billows;
Green mountains, if we will, to bridges give support.
On five sky-scraping Ridges fell our mattocks silver-bright;
O'er the land with three streams our iron arms hold sway.
May we ask the Plague God whither he would take flight?
Burn paper boats with tapers to light his skyward way![4]

• • •

1 The poet imagined the old Southern country with its green hills and blue rivers infected with schistosomiasis germs, with its hamlets devastated by these germs which sucked the blood of peasants like vampires. He seemed to see the earth rotating on its axis and making forty thousand kilometres (eighty thousand li) a day, and revolving around the sun and passing through the Milky Way.

2 A legend said that the poor Cowherd and his wife the Weaver ascended to heaven and became two stars separated by the Milky Way. They could meet each other once a year, on the Double Seventh Day, that is, the seventh day of the seventh lunar month. The poet imagined the Cowherd inquire about the Plague God, that is, schistosomiasis.

3 The crimson rain is the spring rain which falls together with crimson peach petals.

4 To burn paper boats with tapers was a superstitious custom of Chinese peasants in ancient days, who imagined the burned paper boats would carry the God of Plague or Pest away to heaven.

27

七律

到韶山

一九五九年六月

一九五九年六月二十五日到韶山。离别这个地方已有三十二周年了。

别梦依稀咒逝川，
故园三十二年前。
红旗卷起农奴戟，
黑手高悬霸主鞭。
为有牺牲多壮志，
敢教日月换新天。
喜看稻菽千重浪，
遍地英雄下夕烟。

● ● ●

这首诗最早发表在人民文学出版社一九六三年十二月版《毛主席诗词》。

Shaoshan[1] Revisited

June 1959

I visited Shaoshan on June 25, 1959, after an absence of 32 years.

I curse the bygone days which dim as dreams appear:
Thirty-two years ago when I left my homeland,
Red flags aroused the peasants to take up the spear,
While local tyrants brandished high the whip in hand.
More minds grow stronger for the martyrs' sacrifice,
Daring to move the sun and the moon to new skies.
Happy I see now wave on wave of corn and rice;
Here and there heroes come home at dusk as smokes rise.

• • •

1 Shaoshan, situated in the northwest of Xiangtan County, Hunan Province, was the birthplace of Mao Zedong, where he spent his youth, carrying out revolutionary activities and organizing peasant movements until on April 12, 1927, Chiang Kai-shek and the Kuomintang reactionaries suppressed the peasant movement and slaughtered a large number of Communists.

28

七律

登庐山

一九五九年七月一日

一山飞峙大江边，
跃上葱茏四百旋。
冷眼向洋看世界，
热风吹雨洒江天。
云横九派浮黄鹤，
浪下三吴起白烟。
陶令不知何处去，
桃花源里可耕田？

● ● ●

这首诗最早发表在人民文学出版社一九六三年十二月版《毛主席诗词》。

Up Mount Lu[1]

June 1, 1959

A mountain stands in mid-air by the riverside;
Four hundred twists and turns lead to its crest green-dyed.
Cold looks may be cast on the world beyond the sea;
Warm winds sprinkle raindrops on mirrors of the sky.
Clouds cluster o'er nine streams where the yellow crane flies;
Waves roll down three eastern valleys whence smokes rise.
Were the poet Tao still in the Peach-Blossom Village,
Would he not find the fertile land there good for tillage?

• • •

1 Mount Lu is situated in northern Jiangxi, by the side of the Yangtze River. From its summit one might see the Yellow Crane Tower in the west and the factories pouring forth white smoke in the east. Tao Yuanming (365–427) was a poet who lived at the foot of Mount Lu and who would rather retire and plow the fertile land there than be a petty official and bow to his superiors. The Peach-Blossom Village was his utopia, about which he wrote the following poem:

Among the haunts of men I build my cot;
There's noise of wheels and hoofs, but I hear not.
How can it leave upon my mind no trace?
Secluded heart creates secluded place.
I pick fence-side chrysanthemums at will
And leisurely I see the southern hill, (Mount Lu)
Where mountain air is fresh both day and night
And where I find home-going birds in flight.
What is the revelation at this view?
Words fail me e'en if I try to tell you.

29

七绝

为女民兵题照

一九六一年二月

飒爽英姿五尺枪，
曙光初照演兵场。
中华儿女多奇志，
不爱红装爱武装。

● ● ●

这首诗最早发表在人民文学出版社一九六三年十二月版《毛主席诗词》。

Militia Women
—Inscription on a Photo[1]

February 1961

So bright and brave, with rifles five feet long,
At early dawn they shine on drilling place.
Most Chinese daughters have a desire strong
To face the powder, not powder the face.

• • •

1 Many ancient Chinese poems were inscribed on paintings and artwork. When photography appeared, poets started to inscribe their works on them. The "militia woman" in the photo was Li, Mao's secretary.

30

七律

答友人

一九六一年

九嶷山上白云飞，

帝子乘风下翠微。

斑竹一枝千滴泪，

红霞万朵百重衣。

洞庭波涌连天雪，
长岛人歌动地诗。
我欲因之梦寥廓，
芙蓉国里尽朝晖。

● ● ●

这首诗最早发表在人民文学出版社一九六三年十二月版《毛主席诗词》。

Reply to a Friend[1]

1961

Amid sailing white clouds Nine Mysterious Peaks[2] tower;
Riding the wind, two Queens come down from the Green Bower.
Their bamboo canes specked with a thousand tears they shed;
Their pleated dresses made of myriad clouds rose-red.

Dongting's waves surge like snow to level sky and lake;
Long Isle[3] overflows with songs to make the earth shake.
On wings of songs I soar into the wildest dreams
To see a Lotus land[4] bathed in morning sunbeams.

• • •

1 The friend here refers to Zhou Shizhao (1897–1976), schoolmate of Mao Zedong in Hunan.

2 The Nine Mysterious Peaks are also called Changwu Mountains in Hunan Province. A legend said that Emperor Shun died in 2205 BC and was buried at the foot of the Nine Mysterious Mountains, and that the two Queens, daughters of Emperor Yao and wives of Emperor Shun, came to visit his tomb and wept such copious tears that the bamboo all around was specked.

3 The Long Isle is also called Orange Islet in Changsha.

4 A poet of the Five Dynasties, in his poem "A Rainy Night on River Xiang," described Hunan as "The Lotus Land for miles and miles in autumn wind." So Hunan was called "Lotus Land."

31

七绝

为李进同志题所摄庐山仙人洞照

一九六一年九月九日

暮色苍茫看劲松，

乱云飞渡仍从容。

天生一个仙人洞，

无限风光在险峰。

● ● ●

这首诗最早发表在人民文学出版社一九六三年十二月版《毛主席诗词》。

The Immortal's Cave[1]
—Inscription on a Photo Taken by Li Jin

September 9, 1961

A sturdy pine, as viewed in twilight dim and low,
Remains at ease while riotous clouds come and go.
The Fairy Cave's a wonder wrought by Nature's hand:
The view from perilous peak is sublime and grand.

• • •

1 The Immortal's Cave or the Fairy Cave is a rock scenery of Mount Lu in Northern Jiangxi. At an altitude of 1,049 metres, the cave can hold 1,000 persons. At the entrance to the cave there is a huge stone on which are inscribed four big characters: "See sailing clouds here!" On the rock there grows a sturdy pine tree.

32

七律

和郭沫若同志

一九六一年十一月
十七日

一从大地起风雷，
便有精生白骨堆。
僧是愚氓犹可训，
妖为鬼蜮必成灾。

金猴奋起千钧棒，
玉宇澄清万里埃。
今日欢呼孙大圣，
只缘妖雾又重来。

● ● ●

这首诗最早发表在人民文学出版社一九六三年十二月版《毛主席诗词》。

〔附〕 郭沫若原诗

七律·看《孙悟空三打白骨精》

人妖颠倒是非淆，
对敌慈悲对友刁。
咒念金箍闻万遍，
精逃白骨累三遭。
千刀当剐唐僧肉，
一拔何亏大圣毛。
教育及时堪赞赏，
猪犹智慧胜愚曹。

Reply to Comrade Guo Moruo[1]

November 17, 1961

With the rise of the wind-and-thunder storm on earth,
Out of white skeletons a Spirit had its birth.
The Monk might learn a lesson, though a foolish master;
The Spirit, being evil, surely brings disaster.
The Monkey swung his fabulous wand for a sweep;
The jade-like dome was cleared of all dust wide and deep.
We hail the ever-victorious Monkey King today,
For the mist-veiled Spirit is again on his way.

• • •

1 After attending the performance of "The Monkey King Subdues the White Bone Demon," Guo Moruo wrote the following poem condemning the foolish Monk who was kind to the White Bone Demon and unkind to the Monkey King:

The Monk confounded men and demons, right and wrong;
He was unkind to his friend but kind to his foe.
Thousands of times he chanted the Golden Hoop Song[2].
But three times he let the Demon of White Bone go.
The foolish Monk deserved to be torn limb from limb.
Why should the Monkey help him by plucking a hair?
'Tis praise-worthy to give timely lesson to him;
Even the Pig[3] grew wiser than the Monk unfair.

2&3 The Monkey King and the Pig were followers of the Monk, who could cause an awful crashing headache to the Monkey by chanting the Golden Hoop Song.

33

卜算子

咏梅

一九六一年十二月

读陆游咏梅词，反其意而用之。

风雨送春归，
飞雪迎春到。
已是悬崖百丈冰，
犹有花枝俏。

俏也不争春，
只把春来报。
待到山花烂漫时，
她在丛中笑。

这首词最早发表在人民文学出版社一九六三年十二月版《毛主席诗词》。

〔附〕 陆游原词

卜算子·咏梅

驿外断桥边，
寂寞开无主。
已是黄昏独自愁，
更著风和雨。

无意苦争春，
一任群芳妒。
零落成泥碾作尘，
只有香如故。

Tune: Song of Divination

Ode to the Mume Blossom[1]

December 1961

On reading Lu You's "Ode to the Mume Blossom,"[2] I countered it with the following lines.

Then spring depart'd in wind and rain;
With flying snow it's back again.
Though icicles from beetling cliffs still hang miles long,
One flower sweet and fair is thereamong.

Though sweet and fair, with other flowers she won't rival,
But only heralds spring's arrival.
When mountain flowers run riot for miles and miles,
Among them she will be all smiles.

• • •

1 The poem was written by Mao Zedong in December 1961 after he read the Southern Song Dynasty poet Lu You's "Ode to the Mume Blossom"; the two shared the same title and tune. The mume blossom in Lu's poem was tough yet solitary, while Mao depicted it as jovial and beautiful.

China faced its most difficult years after the founding of the People's Republic. By portraying the mume blossom, Mao expressed his faith it would overcome all hardships, all the while never willing to claim the credits for the success himself.

2 Lu You (1125–1210) was a patriotic poet of the Southern Song Dynasty. Of all the flowers he loved the mume blossom most and had written more than one hundred poems about it. One of them reads as follows:

Beside the broken bridge and outside the post-hall,
A flower is blooming forlorn.
Saddened by her solitude at nightfall,
By wind and rain she's further torn.

Let other flowers their envy pour.
To spring she lays no claim.
Fallen in mud and ground to dust, she seems no more.
But her fragrance is still the same.

34

七律

冬云

一九六二年十二月二十六日

雪压冬云白絮飞，
万花纷谢一时稀。
高天滚滚寒流急，
大地微微暖气吹。
独有英雄驱虎豹，
更无豪杰怕熊罴。
梅花欢喜漫天雪，
冻死苍蝇未足奇。

●　●　●

这首诗最早发表在人民文学出版社一九六三年十二月版《毛主席诗词》。

Winter Clouds[1]

December 26, 1962

Like cotton fluff fly winter clouds hard pressed by snow;
All flowers fallen now, for a time few still blow.
In the steep sky cold waves are swiftly sweeping by;
On the vast earth warm winds gradually growing high.
Only heroes can hunt tigers and leopards down;
No brave man will be scared by wild bears black or brown.
Even mume blossoms welcome a skyful of snow;
No wonder flies are frozen to death down below.

• • •

1 Written on the poet's birthday.

35

满江红

和郭沫若同志

一九六三年一月九日

小小寰球，

有几个苍蝇碰壁。

嗡嗡叫，

几声凄厉，

几声抽泣。

蚂蚁缘槐夸大国，

蚍蜉撼树谈何易。

正西风落叶下长安，

飞鸣镝。

多少事，

从来急；

天地转，

光阴迫。

一万年太久，

只争朝夕。

四海翻腾云水怒，

五洲震荡风雷激。

要扫除一切害人虫，

全无敌。

● ● ●

这首词最早发表在人民文学出版社一九六三年十二月版《毛主席诗词》。

〔附〕 郭沫若原词

满江红

沧海横流，
方显出英雄本色。
人六亿，
加强团结，
坚持原则。
天垮下来擎得起，
世披靡矣扶之直。
听雄鸡一唱遍寰中，
东方白。

太阳出，
冰山滴；
真金在，
岂销铄？
有雄文四卷，
为民立极。
桀犬吠尧堪笑止，
泥牛入海无消息。
迎东风革命展红旗，
乾坤赤。

Tune: The River All Red

Reply to Comrade Guo Moruo[1]

January 9, 1963

Upon this globe so small
A few flies are running against the wall.
They hum and squeak,
With pain they shriek,
With spasms they squall.
An ant on a locust would boast 'twas a big country;
A pismire could not find it easy to shake one tree.
At Chang'an[2] the west wind is blowing off leaves dying;
Whistling arrows are flying.

Many deeds should soon be done
At the earliest date.
The earth turns round the sun;
For no man will time wait.
We cannot bear ten thousand years' delay.
Seize but the day!
The four seas are stirred up by angry clouds and waves;
The five continents convulsed by the storm which raves.
Sweep all vermins away.
Invincible for aye!

• • •

1 Guo Moruo's poem reads as follows:

On an angry sea
Our heroes' mettle is tried.
Six hundred million people free,
Strengthen our ties!
By principles abide!
We can shore up the falling skies
And raise men from their knee.
Hear the cock's crow far and wide!
Day breaks on the eastern side.

See the sun rise
And melt mountain ice.
But fire-proof gold
Won't melt away.
Four books[3] so bold
Show us the way.
The tyrant's dogs might bark at a wise king in vain;
The clay ox submerged would not come out again.
In the east wind Revolution's read flag's unfurled,
Red will be the whole world.

2 Chang'an was the capital of China in the Han, Tang and other dynasties.

3 The "four books" refer to the four volumes of *Mao Zedong's Selected Works*.

36

七律

吊罗荣桓同志

一九六三年十二月

记得当年草上飞，
红军队里每相违。
长征不是难堪日，
战锦方为大问题。
斥鷃每闻欺大鸟，
昆鸡长笑老鹰非。
君今不幸离人世，
国有疑难可问谁？

● ● ●

这首诗最早发表在一九七八年九月九日《人民日报》。

Elegy on Comrade Luo Ronghuan[1]

December 1963

I remember then our Red Army men were fleet;
We fought now here now there, so we could hardly meet.
Those days of our Long March were not too hard to bear;
Your battle of Jinzhou was decisive warfare.
A quail in bush may jeer at a high-flying roc;
An eagle sometimes flies e'en lower than a cock.
Now to our deep regret you've left this world for e'er.
With whom can I consult on knotty state affair?

• • •

1 Marshal Luo Ronghuan (1902–1963) was one of the close comrades-in-arms of Mao Zedong. He took part in the Long March in 1934–1935 and won the battle of Jinzhou against Kuomintang forces in 1948. The "high-flying roc" and the "eagle" refer to Luo Ronghuan.

37

贺新郎

读史

一九六四年春

人猿相揖别。
只几个石头磨过，
小儿时节。
铜铁炉中翻火焰，
为问何时猜得，
不过几千寒热。
人世难逢开口笑，
上疆场彼此弯弓月。
流遍了，
郊原血。

一篇读罢头飞雪，
但记得斑斑点点，
几行陈迹。
五帝三皇神圣事，
骗了无涯过客。
有多少风流人物？
盗跖庄蹻流誉后，
更陈王奋起挥黄钺。
歌未竟，
东方白。

●　●　●
这首词最早发表在《红旗》一九七八年第九期。

Tune: Congratulations to the Bridegroom

Reading History

Spring 1964

When man and monkey waved goodbye,
Leaving some tools of the stone age,
It was man's childish stage.
Then bronze and iron melted, flames rose high.
When did man learn the art, you know?
But a few thousand years ago.
Few men exchanged broad smiles instead of blow;
They shot each other on the battlefield with bows.
The plain turned red
With blood they shed.

One book just read,
White hair snowed on my head.
I remember but a few lines,
A few traces and signs.
The sacred deeds of emperors and kings
Deceived so many people for so many springs.
How many of them deserved a real hero's name?
Rebels like Dao Zhi and Zhuang Qiao outdid their fame.
Chen Sheng revolted then[1]
With his axe-wielding men.
Their songs ne'er ceased;
Bright was the east.

• • •

1 Dao Zhi, Zhuang Qiao and Chen Sheng were leaders of peasant uprisings over two thousand years ago.

38

水调歌头

重上井冈山

一九六五年五月

久有凌云志，
重上井冈山。
千里来寻故地，
旧貌变新颜。
到处莺歌燕舞，
更有潺潺流水，
高路入云端。
过了黄洋界，
险处不须看。

风雷动，
旌旗奋，
是人寰。
三十八年过去，
弹指一挥间。
可上九天揽月，
可下五洋捉鳖，
谈笑凯歌还。
世上无难事，
只要肯登攀。

●　●　●

这首词最早发表在《诗刊》一九七六年一月号。

Tune: Prelude to the Melody of Water

Mount Jinggang Reascended[1]

May 1965

Above the clouds I've long aspired to soar,
And so I come up Mount Jinggang once more.
A long trip brings me to my old familiar nook,
Where everything has taken on a new look.
Here orioles sing, there swallows swirl,
O'er there streams purl,
And cloud-capped roads lead to the sky.
But after Huangyangjie,
No perilous place will arrest the eye.

The storm is raging
With flags unfurled:
Such is man's world.
Thirty-eight years are gone
As fast as a fillip is done.
We can bring down the moon from the ninth heaven,
Or catch the giant turtles in the sea,
And come back amid triumphant songs in high glee.
Nothing is hard under the sky
If we but dare to climb up high.

• • •

1 In late May 1965, Mao Zedong revisited Mount Jinggang to sightsee and investigate local livelihoods. He went to Huangyangjie and Ciping to see the water conservancy and road construction projects in Mount Jinggang, as well as to look into local people's lives, having meetings and interviews with former Red Army soldiers, families of martyrs, cadres and common people. There were 38 years between October 1927 and May 1965, when Mao Zedong led his troops after Autumn Harvest Uprising to Mount Jinggang.

39

念奴娇

鸟儿问答

一九六五年秋

鲲鹏展翅，
九万里，
翻动扶摇羊角。
背负青天朝下看，
都是人间城郭。
炮火连天，
弹痕遍地，
吓倒蓬间雀。
怎么得了，
哎呀我要飞跃。

借问君去何方，

雀儿答道：

有仙山琼阁。

不见前年秋月朗，

订了三家条约。

还有吃的，

土豆烧熟了，

再加牛肉。

不须放屁，

试看天地翻覆。

● ● ●

这首词最早发表在《诗刊》一九七六年一月号。

Tune: Charm of a Maiden Singer

Dialogue between Two Birds[1]

Autumn 1965

The roc spreads his wings and flies
Ninety thousand miles, rousing hard
Blowing cyclones. The blue skies
On his back, he looks down
And sees on earth city and town.
With gunfire the sky is loud
And by shells the earth is scarred;
The sparrow in his bush is cowed.
"What can be done? Alas the day!
I want to flit and fly away."

"May I ask where you want to go?"
And the sparrow replies,
"To a fairyland with ivory towers.
But don't you know two years ago
When the moon lit the autumn skies,
A pact was signed by three big powers?
Besides, they have for food
Potatoes cooked and beef well stewed ..."
"Shut up! You bet
Heaven and earth will be upset."

• • •

1 Mao wrote the poem in the autumn of 1965 sarcastically mocking the opportunists in the International Communist Movement. "Potatoes" and "beef" were to ridicule Khrushchev's "goulash" way of "welfare communism" which he proposed in 1964.

In the early 1960s, Sino-Soviet relations became deeply strained, leading to the Soviet Union's withdrawal of all its experts and technicians, which caused great losses to China. On August 5, 1963, the Soviet Union, the US and the UK signed the Treaty Banning Nuclear Weapon Tests in the Atmosphere, in Outer Space and Under Water. This act by the Soviet Union was seen as a betrayal to China.

插　图

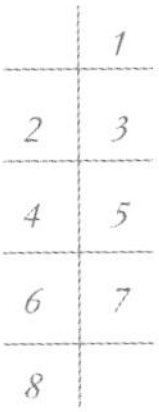

1. 沁园春·长沙　　车鹏飞 绘

2. 采桑子·重阳　　何　曦 绘

3. 浪淘沙·北戴河　　车鹏飞 绘

4. 沁园春·雪　　车鹏飞 绘

5. 七律·送瘟神　　何　曦 绘

6. 七律·答友人　　何　曦 绘

7. 卜算子·咏梅　　何　曦 绘

8. 水调歌头·重上井冈山　　车鹏飞 绘

独立寒秋湘江北去橘子洲头看万山红遍层林尽染漫江碧透百舸争流鹰击长空鱼翔浅底万类霜天竞自由怅寥廓问苍茫大地谁主沉浮携来百侣曾游忆往昔峥嵘岁月稠恰同学少年风华正茂书生意气挥斥方遒指点江山激扬文字粪土当年万户侯曾记否到中流击水浪遏飞舟
毛泽东沁园春长沙

大雨落幽燕白浪滔天秦皇
岛外打鱼船一片汪洋都不
见知向谁边往事越千年
魏武挥鞭东临碣石有遗篇
萧瑟秋风今又是换了人间
毛泽东浪淘沙北戴河

北国风光千里冰封万里
雪飘望长城内外惟余莽莽
大河上下顿失滔滔山舞银蛇原驰
蜡象欲与天公试比高须晴日
看红装素裹分外妖娆江山如
此多娇引无数英雄竞折腰
惜秦皇汉武略输文采唐宗
宋祖稍逊风骚一代天骄成吉
思汗只识弯弓射大雕俱往矣数
风流人物还看今朝

己亥春
何芗畫於海上

己亥春何为於海上訥訥堂

久有凌云志重上井冈山千里来寻故地旧貌变新颜到处莺歌燕舞更有潺潺流水高路入云端过了黄洋界险处不须看风雷动旌旗奋是人寰三十八年过去弹指一挥间可上九天揽月可下五洋捉鳖谈笑凯歌还世上无难事只要肯登攀
毛泽东水调歌头重上井冈山

画家简介

●●●

车鹏飞（1951 年生）

山东莱阳人。毕业于上海师范大学。上海中国画院画师，中国美术家协会会员，上海市美术家协会常务理事。曾任上海中国画院副院长。

何　曦（1960 年生）

浙江嘉兴人。毕业于浙江美术学院。上海中国画院画师、创研室主任，中国美术家协会会员，上海市美术家协会常务理事。

副编

40—63

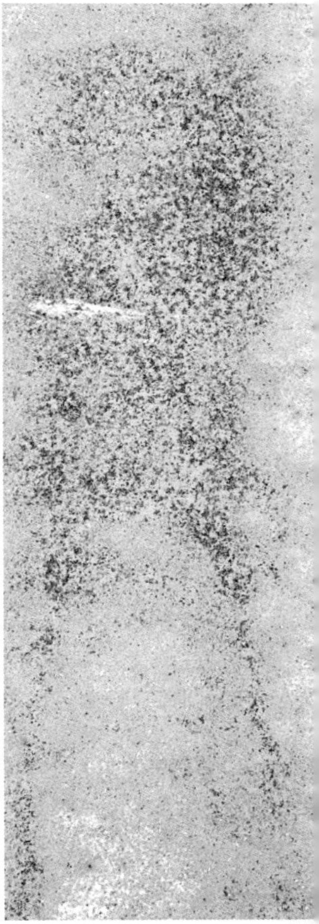

40

五古

挽易昌陶

一九一五年五月

去去思君深，

思君君不来。

愁杀芳年友，

悲叹有余哀。

衡阳雁声彻，

湘滨春溜回。

感物念所欢，

踯躅南城隈。

城隈草萋萋，

涔泪侵双题。

采采余孤景，

日落衡云西。

方期沆瀁游，
零落匪所思。
永诀从今始，
午夜惊鸣鸡。
鸣鸡一声唱，
汗漫东皋上。
冉冉望君来，
握手珠眶涨。
关山蹇骥足，
飞飙拂灵帐。
我怀郁如焚，
放歌倚列嶂。

列嶂青且茜，
愿言试长剑。
东海有岛夷，
北山尽仇怨。
荡涤谁氏子，
安得辞浮贱。
子期竟早亡，
牙琴从此绝。

琴绝最伤情，
朱华春不荣。
后来有千日，
谁与共平生？
望灵荐杯酒，
惨淡看铭旌。
惆怅中何寄，
江天水一泓。

● ● ●

这首诗作者抄录在一九一五年六月二十五日致湘生的信中，随信最早发表在湖南出版社一九九〇年七月版《毛泽东早期文稿》。

Elegy on Yi Changtao[1]

May 1915

Farther away, the deeper I think of you;
However deep, you will not come in view.
Your death grieves me, your friend of younger days;
However long I sigh, my grief still stays.
The Southern Peak is sad with wild geese's song;
By lakeside grievous water flows along.
Can I not at this sight the past recall?
I loiter long by southern city wall.
By city wall the dewy grasses grow
Like bitter tears along my cheeks which flow.
I'm left alone 'mid grass with coloured cloud;
The sun is setting west of mountains proud.

When I did hope we would go far and wide,
Who could foretell you'd wither like grass dried?
From now on I cannot see you again;
Cock's crow at midnight[2] would thrill me with pain.
The cock's first crow reminds me of my friend;
I stroll to the east without aim or end.
I fondly wish you'd come with bygone years;
I wring my hands, my eyes brimful of tears.
Steep mountains hinder a galloping steed;
The whirlwind stirs your funeral screen with speed.
My heart in flame, my grief can't be oppressed;
I roar a song, leaning on mountain crest.

The mountain crest is crimson-red and green;
I would fain try my long sword with edge keen.
In Eastern Ocean there're barbarians;
On Northern Mountains stand tartarians.[3]
Who would be sons so mean or slaves so base
As not to purify their country's face?
But the good lutist died an early death.
How could the broken lute breathe pleasing breath?
The broken lute would break my strong heart-string;
Your rosy face won't bloom again in spring.

Afterwards e'en though there's so many a day,
Who'll go together with me the same way?
Before your coffin I pour a cup of wine,
Gazing on your funeral board, I pine.
Where can I confide my sad thoughts? I sigh
To see deep water under deep blue sky.

• • •

1 Yi Changtao, a native of Hengshan, Hunan and a student of Hunan First Normal School, was classmate and friend of Mao Zedong. Yi died of illness at home in March 1915, and the school held a memorial ceremony for him on May 23. The poem was in memory of Yi.

2 "Cock's crow at midnight" is an allusion to a Chinese legend, in which two young men rose upon hearing the crow of a rooster and practised swordsmanship. Mao was recalling the days when he and Yi shared the same patriotic ambitions.

3 "Barbarians" refers to the Japanese, while "tartarians" refers to the Russians.

41

七古

送纵宇一郎东行

一九一八年四月

云开衡岳积阴止，
天马凤凰春树里。
年少峥嵘屈贾才，
山川奇气曾钟此。
君行吾为发浩歌，
鲲鹏击浪从兹始。
洞庭湘水涨连天，
艟艨巨舰直东指。

无端散出一天愁，
幸被东风吹万里。
丈夫何事足萦怀，
要将宇宙看稊米。
沧海横流安足虑，
世事纷纭从君理。
管却自家身与心，
胸中日月常新美。

名世于今五百年，
诸公碌碌皆余子。
平浪宫前友谊多，
崇明对马衣带水。
东瀛濯剑有书还，
我返自崖君去矣。

● ● ●

这首诗最早非正式地发表在一九七九年《党史研究资料》第十期，是由罗章龙在《回忆新民学会（由湖南到北京）》一文中提供的。

Seeing Luo Zhanglong[1] Off to Japan

1918

Clouds break o'er Southern Mountains and deep gloom's dispelled;
Peaks amid vernal trees look like phoenix and horse.
While young, like Qu and Jia[2] in talent you excelled;
Mountains and streams inspire you with tremendous force.
You're going and I'm singing stirring songs for you;
The giant roc will beat the waves from now and here.
The lake and river stretching skyward out of view;
Your steamer like a warship to the east will steer.
My sorrow for no reason overspreads the sky;
Luckily the east wind blows it to the far-off land.

For nothing burdening his mind a man should sigh
But see the world as if it were a grain of sand.
Don't worry about counter-currents in the sea
And pay no heed to world events in sorry plight.
Take care your body and your soul be pure and free;
And sun and moon e'er shed on your mind a new light.
High fame will last not longer than five hundred years;
The mediocre cannot boast that they are great.

Before Waves-Calming Palace[3] friendly smile appears;
A strip of water severs our land from their strait[4].
I leave the seaside cliff when I see you no more.
Write to me when you wash your sword by Eastern Shore[5]!

• • •

1 Luo Zhanglong (1896–1995) made friend with Mao Zedong when they are both studying in Changsha, Hunan Province. He joined the Communist Party of China in 1921 and was dismissed from the Party in 1931.

2 Qu and Jia refers to Qu Yuan (340–278 BC) and Jia Yi (200–168 BC), both of whom are brilliant talents.

3 Mao Zedong and other friends bade farewell to Luo Zhanglong at the Waves-Calming Palace outside the northern gate of Changsha, Hunan.

4&5 Both the strait and the Eastern Shore refer to Japan.

42

虞美人

枕上

一九二一年

堆来枕上愁何状，
江海翻波浪。
夜长天色总难明，
寂寞披衣起坐数寒星。

晓来百念都灰尽，
剩有离人影。
一钩残月向西流，
对此不抛眼泪也无由。

● ● ●

这首词最早发表在一九九四年十二月二十六日《人民日报》。

Tune: The Beautiful Lady Yu

Written on My Pillow[1]

1921

Like what would sorrow look, piled on my pillows?
A sea of surging billows.
As night is long and dawn is slow to come from afar,
Lonely I rise in nightgown to count star on star.

When morning comes, all thoughts fade from my mind.
How can I leave you far behind?
A hooklike waning moon floats in the western spheres.
At sight of this, can I refrain from shedding tears?

• • •

1 The poet wrote this poem in the summer of 1921 to express how he missed his wife, Yang Kaihui. At this time, Mao went to Shanghai to attend the founding session of the Communist Party, and the newlyweds had to part with each other for some time.

Mao and Yang first met in 1913, and got married in the winter of 1920 after being in love for seven years. Yang then moved into Mao's dormitory in the primary school attached to Hunan First Normal School; the couple held a simple ceremony, with only a single-table dinner to treat their family and closest friends. Yang Kaihui said, "I am fortunate to have my love"; "I believe I was born for him." Such words revealed Yang's affections for Mao, and also his yearning for her.

43

西江月

秋收起义

一九二七年

军叫工农革命，
旗号镰刀斧头。
匡庐一带不停留，
要向潇湘直进。

地主重重压迫，
农民个个同仇。
秋收时节暮云愁，
霹雳一声暴动。

这首词最早非正式地发表在《中学生》一九五六年八月号，是由谢觉哉在题为《关于红军的几首词和歌》的文章中提供的。

Tune: The Moon over the West River

The Autumn Harvest Uprising 1927

Our Army rose for proletarian revolution;
A hammer and a sickle mark our banners red.
From the Lu Mountains[1] we marched with resolution;
To Rivers Xiao and Xiang[2] we fought our way ahead.

The landlords piling up oppressions thick and high;
The peasants bearing common hatred one and all.
The evening clouds look heavy in the autumn sky;
The revolt breaks out as a thunderbolt does fall.

• • •

1 Lu Mountains is situated in the northern part of Jiangxi Province in southeastern China.

2 River Xiang is a river in southern China. The river gave Hunan its Chinese abbreviation, the same as Xiang.

44

六言诗

给彭德怀同志

一九三五年十月

山高路远坑深，
大军纵横驰奔。
谁敢横刀立马？
唯我彭大将军！

● ● ●

这首诗最早发表在一九四七年八月一日《战友报》（冀鲁豫军区政治部主办）。

General Peng Dehuai[1]

October 1935

From east to west by bounds and leaps our army sweeps
All the way over mountains steep and trenches deep.
Who is there wielding his sword and rearing his horse?
It is none but General Peng of our mighty force.

• • •

1 Peng Dehuai (1898–1974) was one of the distinguished leaders of the Red Army. He joined the Communist Party of China in April 1928, led the armed uprising in Pingjiang County, Hunan Province in July, set up the 5th army of the Red Army and led it to Mount Jinggang in November. He took part in the Long March as commander of the 1st Front Army of the Red Army.

45

临江仙

给丁玲同志

一九三六年十二月

壁上红旗飘落照，
西风漫卷孤城。
保安人物一时新。
洞中开宴会，
招待出牢人。

纤笔一枝谁与似？
三千毛瑟精兵。
阵图开向陇山东。
昨天文小姐，
今日武将军。

• • •

这首词最早发表在《新观察》一九八〇第七期。

Tune: Immortal at the River

To Ding Ling[1]

December 1936

On streaming banners red, departing sunbeams fall;
The western wind is whirling round the city wall.
Your presence brightens all of us and brings high glee,
The cave is turned into a banquet hall
To welcome you, a prisoner set free.

Second to none, though delicate your pen appears,
Yet it may brave three thousand musketeers.
East of the mountains Long you go in proud array;
In yesterday's fair writer one reveres
Heroic captain of today.

• • •

1 Ding Ling (1904–1986), woman writer, who joined the Communist Party of China in 1932, was imprisoned by the Kuomintang at Nanjing for more than three years. Set free in the summer of 1936, she went to Bao'an in the northwest of Shaanxi Province, where she was welcomed by Mao Zedong in a cave. Asked about her plan, she said she would serve in the army, and then went to the east of Long Mountains on the border of Shaanxi and Gansu.

46

五律

挽戴安澜将军

一九四三年三月

外侮需人御，
将军赋采薇。
师称机械化，
勇夺虎罴威。
浴血东瓜守，
驱倭棠吉归。
沙场竟殒命，
壮志也无违。

● ● ●

这首诗根据一九四三年戴安澜将军追悼会挽联挽诗登记册刊印。最早非正式地发表在一九八三年十二月二十八日《人民政协报》，是在一篇诠释这首诗典故的文章中提供的。

Elegy on General Dai Anlan[1]

March 1943

We must repel the foreign foe;
Singing martial songs did you go.
Leading Division motorized,
The bears and tigers you despised.
At East Towns you waged bloody fight;
You drove the Japs with main and might.
You gave your life in battlefield,
Your will to serve the State fulfilled.

1 Dai Anlan (1904–1942) was a commander of the Kuomintang. During the Asia-Pacific War which started in December 1941, the government of the Republic of China sent three armies to Burma in order to reinforce the British army, with Dai's division among them. He was 38 years old when he died for his country in May 1942 in northern Burma.

47

五律

张冠道中

一九四七年

朝雾弥琼宇，

征马嘶北风。

露湿尘难染，

霜笼鸦不惊。

戎衣犹铁甲，
须眉等银冰。
踟蹰张冠道，
恍若塞上行。

●　●　●

这首诗根据抄件刊印。

After Leaving Yan'an[1]

1947

The morning mist veils the grey sky;
In northern wind my steed's neigh's lost.
Heavy with dew, no dust can fly;
No crow is startled in hoar frost.

My battledress like armour weighs;
My eyebrows look like silver white.
We came to and fro on our ways,
As if the frontier were in sight.

• • •

1 The poem was composed when Mao was forced to leave Yan'an under the siege of the Kuomintang army, possibly before the Battle of Qinghuabian on March 25, 1947.

In June 1946, after the Anti-Japanese War, the Kuomintang army sieged Communist-controlled areas on the border of Hubei and Henan. This was followed by an all-out civil war. In March 1947, the Kuomintang launched a sudden attack with 140,000 soldiers on Yan'an, Shaanxi, the base of the Communist government and PLA headquarters. With only 20,000 personnel, the Northwestern Field Army fought hard for six days and nights south of Yan'an so as to cover the pullout of the Communist leadership. On the night of March 18, Mao Zedong left Yan'an with last of the staff officers and started his mobile leadership in northern Shaanxi.

48

五律

喜闻捷报

一九四七年

中秋步运河上，闻西北野战军收复蟠龙作。

秋风度河上，
大野入苍穹。
佳令随人至，
明月傍云生。
故里鸿音绝，
妻儿信未通。
满宇频翘望，
凯歌奏边城。

● ● ●

这首诗根据抄件刊印。

Rejoicing over the Victory[1]

1947

On strolling along the canal on Mid-Autumn Festival, I learned of the reclamation of Panlong, and composed the poem.[2]

The river swept by autumn breeze,
The vast plain extends to the sky.
The festival comes as we please:
The moon shines bright, the clouds float by.
No news is brought by the wild geese,
From my homeland and family.
I gaze up on high without cease:
The border town's loud with victory.

• • •

1 Mao Zedong joyously wrote the poem after learning of the victory in Panlong. There was half a year between the pullout from Yan'an on March 18, 1947 and the reclamation of Panlong, a town near Yan'an. During this time, the Northwestern Field Army transitioned from withdrawal to counter-attack. In mid-September, its main force marched south to attack the enemy from behind, regaining Qinghuabian and Panlong, and becoming a menace to the Kuomintang army in Yan'an.

2 编者译。

49

浣溪沙

和柳亚子先生

一九五〇年十一月

颜斶齐王各命前，
多年矛盾廓无边，
而今一扫纪新元。

最喜诗人高唱至，
正和前线捷音联，
妙香山上战旗妍。

● ● ●

这首词最早发表在人民文学出版社一九八六年九月版《毛泽东诗词选》。

Tune: Sand of Silk-Washing Stream

Reply to Mr. Liu Yazi[1]

November 1950

The prince commanded and was commanded to obey;
This contradiction developed from day to day.
Now a new era dawns: the prince was swept away.

To our delight the poet chanting loud comes here,
And news of victory reaches us from the frontier.
How nice the fighting flags in Korea would appear!

• • •

1 At the dance performance of "Doves of Peace" on October 4, 1950, Liu Yazi wrote a poem to the tune of "Sand of Silk-Washing Stream," which begins by the following verse:

White doves of peace dance in splendid array.

Mao Zedong wrote in reply the above poem, in which the same rhyme sequences is used and "the prince" refers to Chiang Kai-shek.

50

七律

和周世钊同志

一九五五年十月

春江浩荡暂徘徊，
又踏层峰望眼开。
风起绿洲吹浪去，
雨从青野上山来。
尊前谈笑人依旧，
域外鸡虫事可哀。
莫叹韶华容易逝，
卅年仍到赫曦台。

● ● ●

这首诗作者抄录在一九五五年十月四日致周世钊的信中，随信最早发表在人民出版社一九八三年十二月版《毛泽东书信选集》。

In Reply to Comrade Zhou Shizhao[1]

October 1955

In spring we loiter by the rolling river's side;
Again we reach the peaks with our eyes open wide.
The wind rises o'er islets green, 'mid waves it drops;
The rain from verdurous fields comes up to mountain tops.
Before wine-cups we talk and laugh still as of yore;
Trifling disputes abroad are but things to deplore.
Do not regret our golden hours of days gone by!
Thirty years passed, again we're on this Terrace high.

• • •

1 Zhou Shizhao (1897–1976), schoolmate of Mao Zedong at the First Normal School in Hunan while young and deputy governor of Hunan Province while old.

51

五律

看山

一九五五年

三上北高峰，
杭州一望空。
飞凤亭边树，
桃花岭上风。
热来寻扇子，
冷去对佳人。
一片飘摇下，
欢迎有晚鹰。

● ● ●

这首诗最早发表在《党的文献》一九九三年第六期。

Mountain Views[1]

1955

Thrice I ascend the Northern Height;
The city seems lost to my sight.
By Phoenix Pavilion trees tower;
The wind sweeps over Mount Peach Flower.
When it's hot, I seek the Fan Hill;
I face Peak Beauty when it's chill.
With wings like floating cloud so free,
At dusk Mount Eagle welcomes me.

• • •

1 Being an aged man of 62, Mao Zedong was in Hangzhou working and relaxing at the end of the summer in 1955. Because of Mao's age and health, the doctor advised him to take more exercise such as swimming, hiking and dancing. Therefore, Mao repeatedly visited some famous hills and mountains around West Lake, viewing the beauty of the lake and leaving several improvised poems, with "Mountain Views" one of them.

52

七绝

莫干山

一九五五年

翻身复进七人房，
回首峰峦入莽苍。
四十八盘才走过，
风驰又已到钱塘。

● ● ●

这首诗最早发表在《党的文献》一九九三年第六期。

Mount Mogan[1]

1955

Re-entering the seven-seated carriage, I
Look back and find the peaks melt into the blue sky.
From the forty-eight twists and turns we've just come
down,
My wind-driven car arrives at the lakeside town.

• • •

1 The poem was composed during the same period as "Mountain Views"—when Mao was in Hangzhou. Mount Mogan is part of the Tianmu mountain range in Zhejiang, and is named after the husband and wife swordsmiths Gan Jiang and Mo Ye, who lived in the State of Wu during the Spring and Autumn Period. According to Chinese legend, the couple forged swords in this mountain for Helü, King of Wu. However, the blast furnace failed to melt the metal. Mo Ye suggested that there was insufficient human qi in the furnace so the couple cut their hair and nails and cast them into the furnace, while 300 children helped to blow air with the bellows. The desired result was achieved after three years and the two swords were named after the couple.

Though not very high, Mount Mogan is pleasing, with its forests and springs, which make it an excellent place for spending summertime.

53

七绝

五云山

一九五五年

五云山上五云飞，
远接群峰近拂堤。
若问杭州何处好，
此中听得野莺啼。

● ● ●

这首诗最早发表在《党的文献》一九九三年第六期。

The Rainbow Cloud Mountain[1]

1955

Over the Rainbow Cloud Mountain rainbow clouds fly,
O'ershadow distant peaks and caress the lake nearby.
If you ask me where I would like to linger long,
It's here where I may listen to orioles' song.

• • •

1 The poem was written in the same period as "Mountain Views" and "Mount Mogan;" the three constitute Mao's series of "Mountains in Hangzhou." Mount Wuyun (literally Mountains of the Five-Coloured Clouds), got its name from the clouds coloured cyan, white, dark, crimson, and gold, that are said to swathe the range of five peaks located ten kilometres southwest of downtown Hangzhou. The Qiantang River lies to the south of it, and West Lake to the north. There is an ancient temple named Yunqi in the mountains.

54

七绝

观潮

一九五七年九月

千里波涛滚滚来，
雪花飞向钓鱼台。
人山纷赞阵容阔，
铁马从容杀敌回。

●　●　●

这首诗最早发表在《党的文献》一九九三年第六期。

Watching the Tidal Rise[1]

September 1957

Waves upon waves roll on for miles and miles;
Snowflakes on flakes fall on the fishing site.
A mountain of faces break into broad smiles;
With ease come back rows of battle steeds white.

• • •

1 The tide here refers to the tide of the Qiantang River near Hangzhou. On September 11, 1957, Mao Zedong went from Hangzhou to Yanguan Town, Haining County, Zhejiang, in order to view this renowned tidal wave.

55

七绝

刘蕡

一九五八年

千载长天起大云，

中唐俊伟有刘蕡。

孤鸿铩羽悲鸣镝，

万马齐喑叫一声。

● ● ●

这首诗根据作者审定的抄件刊印。

Liu Fen[1]

1958

A thousand years ago bright cloud rose in dark sky:
Liu Fen dared to defy eunuchs in power high.
A featherless swan hit by arrows could not fly;
All horses mute, alone a steed would voice a cry.

• • •

1 Liu Fen (?–842), born in Changping of You Prefecture (today's Beijing), lived during the Tang Dynasty and is recorded in both the *New Book of Tang* and *Old Book of Tang*. After taking the throne, Emperor Wenzong of Tang started holding exams in the year 828 to select the talented and virtuous. Liu was the only one who boldly expostulated and offered sincere advice that was directly to the point. However, while the eunuchs dominated all authority, the examiner dared not recruit Liu. Liu was unable to serve in an important position all his life; he was framed by the eunuchs and finally died in the Chu area remote from his homeland. Mao Zedong thought highly of Liu's advice and solutions.

56

七绝

屈原

一九六一年秋

屈子当年赋楚骚，
手中握有杀人刀。
艾萧太盛椒兰少，
一跃冲向万里涛。

● ● ●

这首诗根据作者审定的抄件刊印。

Qu Yuan[1]

Autumn 1961

Qu Yuan had rhymed his griefs long, long ago;
He had no sword in hand to kill the foe.
Wild weeds o'ergrown, few sweet flowers could blow;
He plunged into endless waves to end his woe.

• • •

1 Qu Yuan (c. 340–278 BC) was a patriotic poet and an aristocrat of the State of Chu. He served as an official under King Huai of Chu, but was removed from his position after being slandered. During the reign of King Xiang of Chu, Qu Yuan was exiled to River Xiang, where he wrote "Sorrow after Departure," "Jiu Zhang " and "Jiu Ge," before finally drowning himself.

57

七绝二首

纪念鲁迅八十寿辰

一九六一年

其一

博大胆识铁石坚，
刀光剑影任翔旋。
龙华喋血不眠夜，
犹制小诗赋管弦。

其二

鉴湖越台名士乡，
忧忡为国痛断肠。
剑南歌接秋风吟，
一例氤氲入诗囊。

●　●　●

这两首诗根据抄件刊印。

On the 80th Anniversary of Lu Xun's Birthday[1]

1961

I

Broad and brave, firm as steel or stone, with deep insight,
You came into the shade or amid the swords bright.
When blood was shed at Dragon Tower[2] on sleepless night[3],
You played on lute and strings to sing the martyrs' plight.

II

The southern lakeside land teemed with celebrities;
Their heart would break for national calamities.
The cavalier's[4] wind and the heroine's[5] autumn rain
Evaporated like cloud into poetic strain.

• • •

1 Lu Xun (1881–1936), born in Shaoxing, Zhejiang, was a great man of letters, an ideologist, and a revolutionary. Mao Zedong was a lifelong admirer of Lu Xun.

2 Dragon Tower is a place in the suburbs of Shanghai. It was notorious as a killing field.

3 "sleepless night" refers to the night of February 7, 1931, when the Five Martyrs of the League of Left-Wing Writers were executed at Dragon Tower. Lu Xun wrote a poem in memory of them.

4 "cavalier" refers to Lu You, a patriotic poet of China's Southern Song Dynasty.

5 "heroine" refers to Qiu Jin, a modern revolutionist who advocated the overthrow of the Qing Dynasty. She composed the "Song of Autumn Wind":

> All grasses yellow at the autumn breeze's song;
> The autumn wind by nature's vigorous and strong.
> It makes all flowers drop their head with sere leaves lost;

Alone chrysanthemums can stand against the frost.
Flowers in full bloom, they belong to yellow race;
Petal on petal, they transform the country's face.
The mirror-like full moon brightens the river clear.
How can't the river, wave on wave, shiver with fear?
Last night was full of autumn wind and autumn rain;
And autumn frost and autumn dew seem to complain.
The leaves no longer green fear to fall in the breeze;
The immigrating birds bewail atop the trees.
When autumn comes, the weather is so sad and drear,
And autumn thoughts prevail on old Cathay's frontier.
Beyond the border horses are ready to fight;
The angry general puts on golden armour bright.
In golden armour he fights against Hunnish foe;
Millions of Hunnish soldiers, beaten, backward go.
The general laughs and his soldiers rise at his call
To drink to Freedom at the Hunnish capital.

58

杂言诗

八连颂

一九六三年八月一日

好八连，
天下传。
为什么？
意志坚。
为人民，
几十年。
拒腐蚀，
永不沾。
因此叫，
好八连。
解放军，
要学习。
全军民，
要自立。

不怕压，
不怕迫。
不怕刀，
不怕戟。
不怕鬼，
不怕魅。
不怕帝，
不怕贼。
奇儿女，
如松柏。
上参天，
傲霜雪。
纪律好，
如坚壁。

军事好，
如霹雳。
政治好，
称第一。
思想好，
能分析。
分析好，
大有益。
益在哪？
团结力。
军民团结如一人，
试看天下谁能敌。

● ● ●

这首诗最早发表在一九八二年十二月二十六日《解放军报》。

Ode to the Eighth Company[1]

August 1, 1963

Company Eight
Known far and near.
Well known for what?
For its firm will.
Serving the people
Many a year,
Amid corruptions
Unstained still.
So it is called
Company good.
Our people's army,
Learn from it you should.
All ranks and files,
Be self-reliant!

Of all oppressions
Be e'er defiant!
You should not fear
Or sword or spear!
Fear nor the ghosts
Nor the vampires,
Nor the enemy,
Nor the empires!
Ye sons are fine
Like cold-proof pine
Which pierces skies
And snow defies.
Well disciplined,
Firm as a wall,
You're brave and fast,
Like thunder blast.

Putting politics
First, above all,
Good at thinking,
Analyse you could.
Analysis
Will do much good.
What good at length?
Union is strength.
Army and people united as one,
We are unrivaled 'neath the sun.

• • •

1 The Eighth Company was a PLA company stationed on Nanjing Road in Shanghai in May 1949. Over the years in the crowded downtown Shanghai, all its soldiers and staff preserved their diligence and thrifty, generosity and honesty. Mao wrote the poem on the Army Day of 1963 to inspire the company.

59

念奴娇

井冈山

一九六五年五月

参天万木，
千百里，
飞上南天奇岳。
故地重来何所见，
多了楼台亭阁。
五井碑前，
黄洋界上，
车子飞如跃。
江山如画，
古代曾云海绿。

弹指三十八年，

人间变了，

似天渊翻覆。

犹记当时烽火里，

九死一生如昨。

独有豪情，

天际悬明月，

风雷磅礴。

一声鸡唱，

万怪烟消云落。

● ● ●

这首词最早发表在人民文学出版社一九八六年九月版《毛泽东诗词选》。

Tune: Charm of a Maiden Singer

Mount Jinggang[1]

May 1965

Sky-scraping trees
Extend a thousand lis
And fly up to the towering southern peak.
What have I seen when I come to seek
My old familiar places
But new pavilions and terraces?
Before the monument of the Five Wells
And formidable citadels
So steep
The carriage seems to leap.
The scenery the mountain displays
Was a blue sea in ancient days.

Thirty-eight years have gone by
In the twinkling of an eye.
The despot overthrown,
The sky was turned upside down.
I still remember 'mid the beacon fire
The life-and-death struggle which drew nigher and nigher.
It seems to be but yesterday.
Only true heroes could hold sway
Like the bright moon hanging in the sky
Or the thunder-storm raging on high.
When cocks crow loud,
All monsters disappear like smoke or cloud.

• • •

1 "Mount Jinggang" is the companion work of "Mount Jinggang Reascended," both written during Mao Zedong's visit to the mountain in May 1965.

60

七律

洪都

一九六五年

到得洪都又一年，
祖生击楫至今传。
闻鸡久听南天雨，
立马曾挥北地鞭。

鬓雪飞来成废料，
彩云长在有新天。
年年后浪推前浪，
江草江花处处鲜。

● ● ●

这首诗最早发表在一九九四年十二月二十六日《人民日报》。

Nanchang, Capital of Jiangxi[1]

1965

One year has passed, again I come to Nanchang in south;
The deeds on the middlestream[2] still spread from mouth to mouth.
We rose at cockcrow, sword in hand, in southern rain;
We reared our steeds by wielding whips on northern plain.

Useless am I now, age snows on my head hair white.
But radiant clouds will ever make new heaven bright.
The waves will push each other on from year to year;
Riverside grass and flowers ever fresh will appear.

• • •

1 When touring southern China in 1965, Mao Zedong revisited Mount Jinggang and left two pieces of ci lyrics to mark the visit. Mao also stopped at Nanchang since it is not far from Mount Jinggang, and this poem marks his visit to Nanchang.

2 The deeds on the middlestream refers to a tale about Zu Ti (266–321), who served as a court official in the late Western Jin Dynasty. He moved to the south during times of turbulence, and was appointed to a prefectural position in Yuzhou by Emperor Yuan of Jin. When commanding a troop in a northern expedition, he struck the oars on the middlestream, swearing to take back the Central Plains.

61

七律

有所思

一九六六年六月

正是神都有事时，
又来南国踏芳枝。
青松怒向苍天发，
败叶纷随碧水驰。

一阵风雷惊世界，
满街红绿走旌旗。
凭阑静听潇潇雨，
故国人民有所思。

● ● ●

这首诗根据作者审定的抄件刊印。

Yearning[1]

June 1966

It's time in capital for a dream to come true;
Again I tread in southern land 'mid trees in bloom.
Green pines stretch arms in wrath like bolt into the blue;
Withered leaves flow away with running waves in gloom.
A gust of stormy wind would startle men in power;
All streets are red and green with banners fluttering.
Leaning on balustrade, I listen to the shower:
My countrymen are yearning for another spring.

• • •

1 As can be seen from the title "Yearning," the poem concerns worries and thoughts.

In February 1966, An Outline of the Report of Current Academic Discussion (also known as February Outline) was issued after requesting Mao's instructions in Wuhan. However, Mao Zedong in some talks at the end of February, criticized that the February Outline confused right and wrong, and blurred the boundaries between different classes.

In May, the Central Politburo of the CPC held a meeting, comprehensively denying the February Outline, and re-established a Cultural Revolution Group.

In June 1966, an editorial was published by the *People's Daily*, followed by a wave of destruction of the "Four Olds," the establishment of the "Four News," as well as the seizing of and struggling by school principals and teachers. The Great Cultural Revolution hence extended from school to the whole of society, and ten years of chaos started thereupon.

62

七绝

贾谊

贾生才调世无伦，
哭泣情怀吊屈文。
梁王堕马寻常事，
何用哀伤付一生。

• • •

这首诗根据抄件刊印。

Jia Yi[1]

Jia Yi the scholar had a talent without peer;
He mourned by lakeside o'er the exiled poet dear.
What had the student's death to do with the wise master?
Why should he die of grief o'er the prince's disaster?

• • •

1 The poem was not inscribed with a composing date; it was possibly written after the establishment of the People's Republic of China. Jia Yi (200–168 BC) is the only person praised by Mao with two poems.

Jia was a talented youth in Luoyang. He was appointed to a high official position at the age of twenty by Emperor Wen of Han Dynasty, but then was slandered and banished to Changsha in 176 BC. On his way to Changsha, Jia Yi passed River Xiang and wrote "Lament to Qu Yuan" as a sacrificial offering to the patriotic poet. In 174 BC, Jia was recalled by the emperor and served as a tutor for Prince Huai of Liang, who was the beloved youngest son of Emperor Wen. Unfortunately, the prince fell from a horse and lost his life. Though Emperor Wen did not blame Jia, Jia suffered deep guilt and finally died at the young age of 33.

63

七律

咏贾谊

少年倜傥廊庙才，
壮志未酬事堪哀。
胸罗文章兵百万，
胆照华国树千台。
雄英无计倾圣主，
高节终竟受疑猜。
千古同惜长沙傅，
空白汨罗步尘埃。

● ● ●

这首诗根据抄件刊印。

On Jia Yi[1]

While young, he had the talent of serving the State;
To our regret, his ambition was not fulfilled.
He knew the way of commanding an army great,
Of strengthening the State by weakening lords self-willed.
Brave as he was, he could not persuade the king;
Loyal although he was, he fell into disgrace.
Master in Changsha, he's deplored from spring to spring.
Why should he follow, oh! the exiled poet's trace?

• • •

1 "On Jia Yi" is the companion work of "Jia Yi." It can be deducted from the contents and the historical background that both pieces were composed in the same period.

原译序

毛泽东说：诗要“精炼、大体整齐、押韵。”（见1977年12月31日《人民日报》）鲁迅说：“新诗先要有节调，押大致相近的韵，给大家容易记，又顺口，唱得出来。”（见《鲁迅书信集》635页）我以为不但是写诗，译诗也该如此。

鲁迅在《汉文学史纲要》第一篇《自文字至文章》中说：“诵习一字，当识形音义三：口诵耳闻其音，目察其形，心通其义，三识并用，一字之功乃全。其在文章，……遂具三美：意美以感心，一也；音美以感耳，二也；形美以感目，三也。”我以为译诗也要尽可能传达原文的意美、音美、形美。

《毛泽东给陈毅同志谈诗的一封信》中说：“又诗要

用形象思维，不能如散文那样直说。”“形象思维”也是意美；“大体整齐”也是形美；“押韵”也是音美。

有个外国作家说过：“Prose is words in the best order; poetry is the best words in the best order.”（散文是井然有序的文字；诗是井然有序的绝妙好词。）我觉得：“绝妙好词”就是具备意美、音美、形美的文字。

毛泽东诗词是具备意美、音美、形美的艺术高峰。翻译毛泽东诗词也要尽可能传达原诗的三美。

“三美”的基础是“三似”：意似、音似、形似。“意似”就是要传达原文的内容，不能错译、漏译、多译。例如《广昌路上》中的名句：“头上高山，风卷红旗过大关。”原来是写雪里行军，红旗冻得风吹不动，所以毛泽东的手稿写的是“风卷红旗冻不翻”，后来才改成“过大关”的。这一个“卷”字，写出了和严寒作斗争的艰苦。但是现已出版的译本，却把“卷”字译成 unfurl，flutter，wave，flap，都和原文意思相反，理解为“红旗迎风飘扬”了，所以都是误译，不如改成：

O'erhead loom crags;

We go through the strong pass with wind-frozen red flags.

至于多译、漏译，例如有的译本把“风展红旗如画”译成：

Red flags stream in the wind in a blaze of glory.

就增加了一些原文所没有的意思，不如译为：

The wind unrolls red flags like scrolls.

又如“忆往昔峥嵘岁月稠”，译成：

Vivid yet those crowded months and years.

Crowded 这个字如果是译“稠”字，那么“峥嵘”两个字就没有译出来；如果是兼译“峥嵘”，那力量又太弱了。这些例子都没有做到“意似”，当然也就不能传达原文的“意美”。

一般来说，“意似”和“意美”是一致的。例如《贺新郎》中“挥手从兹去”如用英文 wave goodbye 这个短语，就可以说既是“意似”，又传达了原文的“意美”。但是有时“意似”和“意美”却有矛盾，也就是说，“意似”并不一定能传达原文的“意美”。例如“人间正道是沧桑”，有的译本译成“But in man's world seas change into mulberry fields.”这可以说是“意似”的，却没有传达原诗的“意美”。

“意美”有时是历史的原因或者是联想的缘故造成的。译成另外一种语言，没有相同的历史原因，就引不起相同的联想，也就不容易传达原诗的“意美”。因此，在译诗的时候，要充分利用外国诗人的名句和词汇，使之

"洋为中用"。马克思曾要求作家"更加莎士比亚化"(见《马克思恩格斯选集》第四卷 340 页)。莎士比亚的名剧《麦克佩斯》中说:

New sorrows strike heaven on the face.

翻译"天兵怒气冲霄汉"时,不妨借用一部分。莎士比亚的名剧《奥赛罗》中有一句:

The chidden billow seems to pelt the clouds.

也不妨加以修改,借来翻译"白浪滔天"。英国诗人拜仑(Byron)的名诗中有

When we two parted

In silence and tears,

翻译《咏梅》词中的"风雨送春归"就可以效法。英国诗人雪莱(Shelley)的《西风歌》中有"wild west wind",《云雀歌》中有"the sunken sun",翻译《娄山关》中的"西风烈"和"残阳如血"时,也不妨引用,可能更好传达原词的"意美"。

毛泽东诗词中有些"意美"的词汇在英语中找不到"意似"的译文,这种"意美"有时还是"音美"或"形美"造成的。如"烂漫""翩跹""依稀"等都是叠韵,具有"音美"。"沉浮""峥嵘""逶迤"每两个字的偏旁都是一样的,具有"形美"。"磅礴""慷慨"都是双声,

而且偏旁相同，既有“音美”，又有“形美”。“苍茫”“葱茏”不但都是叠韵，而且字头相同，也是“音美”“形美”兼而有之。

怎样才能传达这些有声有色、捉摸不定的绝妙好词的“意美”呢？例如“待到山花烂漫时”，有的译文是“When the mountain flowers are in full bloom”，虽然也可以说是“意似”了，但是没有表达原文如火如荼的形象，不如译为：

When with blooming flowers the mountain is aflame[1]

更加绘声绘色。又如“五岭逶迤腾细浪，乌蒙磅礴走泥丸。”“逶迤”译成 serpentine 可以说是“意似”，而且传达了原文的“意美”；“细浪”译成 rippling rills 更可以使人如闻“细浪”之声，如见“逶迤”之形，加强了译文的“意美”。“磅礴”二字在这里可以考虑译成 pompous，不但有华而不实之意，而且声音也和“磅礴”相近；虽然这字一般不用于山，但在这里可否破格借用一下？“泥丸”如果译成 mud pills，可以说是“意似”，但是没有“意美”，不如改为英美人喜见乐闻的形式 mole-hills，也许更能传达原文的“意美”。

总而言之，要传达毛泽东诗词的“意美”，可以选

1 译序中的译文版本与正文有不一致的情况，这里均未作改动。

择和原文“意似”的“绝妙好词”，可以借用英美诗人喜见乐闻的词汇，还可以借助“音美”“形美”来表达原文的“意美”。

诗要有节调，押韵、顺口、好听，这就是诗词的音美。毛泽东诗词讲究平仄；译成英语可以考虑用抑扬格和扬抑格，也可以用抑抑扬格或扬抑抑格。中国诗主要是七言和五言；七言译成英语可以考虑用亚力山大体，也就是指每行十二个音节的抑扬格诗句；五言可以考虑用英雄体，也就是指每行十个音节的抑扬格诗句。这是个人的主观意见，能否做到，要看客观实践。例如“风雨送春归”，英语译成 Then spring depart'd in wind and rain，可以说是八个音节、四个抑扬格的音步。

至于押韵，最好能够做到“音似”，如《蒋桂战争》上半段四个仄韵“变”“战”“怨”“现”，如果译成 rain，again，pain，vain，就可以说是和原文“大致相近”了。又如“今又重阳，战地黄花分外香”。如果译成：

Again the Double Ninth is coming round,

How sweet are yellow flowers on the battleground![1]

round，ground 和原韵“阳”“香”也可以说是“大致相近”。再如“不周山下红旗乱”，如果用 run riot 这个短语来译，而且把 run 放在句末，那几乎可以说是“音似”

了。不过我觉得最难译得“音似”的，还是“战士指看南粤，更加郁郁葱葱”。如果译成：

Our warriors, pointing south, see Guandong loom

In a richer green and a lusher gloom.

那么最后一行的 green 和 gloom 都是 [g] 的头韵，接着辅音 [r] 和 [l] 配对，[n] 和 [m] 成双，长元音 [i:] 和 [u:] 也很对称。richer 和 lusher 两个字也是辅音 [r] 和 [l] 配对，[tʃ] 和 [ʃ] 成双，短元音 [i] 对 [ʌ] 也算和谐，最后还重复了短元音 [ə]。加上 richer green 两字又有辅音 [r] 的重复，短长元音 [i][i:] 的搭配；lusher gloom 也有辅音 [l] 的重复，短长元音的搭配，听起来多少可以传达一点原文“郁郁葱葱”的“音美”，而“gloom”和“葱”字还可以说是有点“音似”。

以上举的是“音美”和“音似”基本一致的例子。不过“音美”和“音似”矛盾的时候远远超过了一致的时候，这就是说，传达原文的“音美”往往不能做到、甚至也不必做到“音似”，翻译汉语的叠字尤其是如此。

毛泽东诗词中的叠字很丰富，而翻译叠字不但传达“音美”困难，传达“意美”也不容易。《黄鹤楼》这首词只有八行，却用了四对叠字：“茫茫”“沉沉”“苍苍”“滔滔”，而前两对叠字还是对称的，不但具有“音美”，而且具有“形美”，翻译很不容易传达原文的“三美”。Boyd 把“茫茫”译成“wide, wide”，传达了原文的“意美”和“音美”，但把“沉沉”译成“deep, deeply scored”，就没有传达原诗的“形美”。伦敦译本用了“broad, broad”“deep, deep”，倒传达了原文的“形美”，但是“意美”不如用“wide，wide”。至于“烟雨莽苍苍，龟蛇锁大江”，英译文都没有译出“苍苍”的“音美”。我想英文如果译成：

Shrouded in grizzling mist and drizzling rain

似乎更能勾画出蒙蒙灰雾和淋淋细雨的形象。

至于“滔滔”二字，毛泽东诗词中出现过三次：“把酒酹滔滔”“顿失滔滔”和“过眼滔滔云共雾”。“顿失滔滔”还是和“惟余莽莽”对称的，又是一个传达“三美”的问题。我想这两行可以译成：

The boundless land is clad in white;

The endless waves are lost to sight.

用两个字尾相同的形容词来译这两对叠字，也许可能传达一点原文的“音美”。译文形容词对形容词，名词对名词，动词对动词，短语对短语，也可以传达原文的“形美”。“过眼滔滔云共雾”要和上一行“知误会前番书语”合译：

The misunderstanding arose from what I wrote,

But it will melt like clouds that fleet and mists that float.

这就是用 fleet 和 float 两个双声字来译叠字了。有时叠字分开，如“不爱红装爱武装”，需要巧译如下：

Most Chinese daughters have a desire strong

To face the powder, not powder the face.

总而言之，要传达毛泽东诗词的“音美”，可以借用英美诗人喜见乐用的格律，选择和原文“音似”的韵脚，还可以借助于“双声”“叠韵”“重复”等方法来表达原文的“音美”。

关于诗词的“形美”，主要是“长短”和“对称”两个问题，最好能够做到“形似”，至少也要做到“大体整齐”。例如《十六字令》之三：“山，刺破青天锷未残。天欲堕，赖以拄其间。”如果译成英语：

Peaks

Piercing the blue without blunting the blade,

The sky would fall

But for this colonnade.

原文十六个字，译文也是十六个字；原文四行的字数分别是一、七、三、五字，译文如果把第三行最后一个字移到下一行，那就和原文长短一样，完全“形似”。不过译文各行的音节数分别是一、十、四、六个，也可以说是和原文基本“音似”了。

一般说来，要求译文和原文“形似”或“音似”都是很难做到的，只能要求大体近似。例如“多少事，从来急；天地转，光阴迫”。原文每行三字，短促有力，充分表达了急迫的内容。译文如果也要译成每行三字或者三个音节，那就很难；我想译成三四个字或四到六个音节，就可以算是“大体整齐”。如：

(1) So many deeds
Bear no delay.
Sun and earth turn,
Time flies away.

(2) So many things
Should soon be done.
Sun and earth turn,
Time waits for none.

(3) With so much to do,
We must e'er make haste.
As sun and earth turn,
There's no time to waste.

(4) Many deeds should soon be done

At the earliest date.

The earth turns round the sun;

For no man will time wait.

第一种译文每行基本三字，四个音节；第二种译文每行基本四字，也是四个音节；第三种译文每行基本五字，五个音节；第四种译文却是六个音节，但第一、三行押韵，第二、四行也押韵，在传达原文“形美”的时候，还兼顾了“音美”。这四种译文都可以说是“大体整齐”。

至于对仗，毛泽东诗中用的很多，七律的第三行和第四行，第五行和第六行，都是对仗工整的；就是词中的对仗也不少，前面已经举了“惟余莽莽”和“顿失滔滔”的例子。这里再来补充一个诗例：“高天滚滚寒流急，大地微微暖气吹”。不但对仗工整，而且叠字有力。我想如果译成：

In the steep sky cold waves are swiftly sweeping by;

On the vast earth warm winds gradually growing high.

那不但是状语对状语，主、谓语对主、谓语，而且用了 sw 的双声来译“滚滚”，用了 gr 的双声来译“微微”，可以说是基本传达了原文的意美、音美和形美。

同时传达“三美”很不容易，最好能把传达“音美”

和“形美”的困难分散。例如《送瘟神》第二首第三至八行是：“红雨随心翻作浪，青山着意化为桥。天连五岭银锄落，地动三河铁臂摇。借问瘟君欲何往，纸船明烛照天烧。”如果译成：

The vernal wind awakens myriads of willows;
Six hundred million are masters of wisest sort.
Crimson rain, as we wish, turns into fertile billows;
Green mountains, if we will, to bridges give support.
Our iron arms remoulding three streams rock the land;
Our silver mattocks felling five peaks rend the sky.
Where will the God of Plague take flight? Burn tapers and
Paper boats to throw light upon his way on high!

这样，第三行和第一行押韵，第四行和第二行押韵，第五行和第七行押韵，第六行和第八行押韵，把传达音韵的困难由第一、二、七、八行分担了一半，第三至六行就可以集中力量来传达原文的节奏和对仗了。

总而言之，要传达毛泽东诗词的“形美”，主要是在句子长短方面和对仗工整方面，尽量做到“形似”。不过这里应该说明一下：在“三美”之中，“意美”是最重要的，第一位的；“音美”是次要的，是第二位的；“形美”是更次要的，是第三位的。我们要在传达原文“意美”的前提下，尽可能传达原文的“音美”；还要在传达原文“意美”和“音美”的前提下，尽可能传达原文的“形美”；努力做到“三美”齐备。如果三者不能得兼，那么，首先可以不要求“形似”，也可以不要求“音似”；但是无论如何，都要尽可能传达原文的“意美”和“音美”。

如果两个词汇都能传达原文的“意美”，其中有一个还能传达原文的“音美”，那么翻译的时候，当然是选择兼备“音美”的词汇。即使一个词汇只能传达八分“意美”和八分“音美”，那也比另一个能传达九分“意美”和五分“音美”的词汇强。例如“风展红旗如画”中的“展”字，如果译成 unfurl，可能比 unroll 好一点；但是 unroll 能和 scroll 押韵，unfurl 却只有节奏而没有韵，总的看来，不如 unroll。因此 unroll 在“意美”和“音美”两方面的总分加起来比 unfurl 高；而我认为总分最高的词汇就是 the best word（绝妙好词）。

毛泽东诗词的译文在世界各国广泛流传。就以英译文而论，据我所知，至少已经出版了 11 种译本：

1. 我国 1958 年出版的 Andrew Boyd 的译本；

2. 英国 1965 年出版的 Michael Bullock and Jerome Ch'en 的合译本；

3. 香港 1966 年出版的 Dr. Wong Man 的译本；

4. 美国1972年出版的聂华苓和Paul Engle的合译本;

5. 美国 1972 年出版的 Willis Barnstone 的译本；

6. 我国外文出版社 1976 年的译本；

7. 南京大学 1978 年出版的《毛主席诗词三十九首》；

8. 洛阳外国语学院 1978 年出版的《毛主席诗词四十二首》；

9. 湖南人民出版社 1980 年出版的《毛泽东诗词》；

10. 香港三联书店 1980 年出版的林同端英译本；

11. 香港商务印书馆 1981 年出版的许渊冲译《中国现代革命家诗词选》中有毛泽东诗词四十三首。

美国聂译本的序言中说："《毛泽东诗词》（到 1972 年）据说已经发行了 5700 万册，发行量之大，超过了全世界任何诗人的诗集，几乎等于有史以来出版过的英文诗集的总和。"由此可见毛泽东诗词在国内外的影响之大。1986 年，我国又出版了《毛泽东诗词选》，共选入诗词 50 首。今年是毛泽东 100 周年诞辰，为了纪念这位巨人的丰功伟绩，中国对外翻译出版公司决定出版《毛泽东诗词选》新英译本。英国诗人白英说过："了解一个民族，最好通过诗歌，而中国人有史以来一直把诗看成文化的瑰宝。"因此，我想，《毛泽东诗词选》新译本的出版，会使英语世界对这位伟人、对他所继承发扬了的中国文化，有“更上一层楼”的了解。

美国哥伦比亚大学出版的《中国诗选》说：“从某种意义上讲，如果没有中国诗词，没有中国诗的影响，我们想象不出本世纪英诗的面目。”《诗选》的英译者华逊教授说：“现在，有些中国诗的英译者继续向更自由的方向发展，有些译者却在实践中重新运用以前舍弃了的韵脚和格律。我个人相信，各种各样的改革和实践都值得欢迎，因为通过改革实践，才有希望发现更有效的方法，使中国诗词的‘美’化为英文。”因此，我希望《毛泽东诗词选》新译本的问世，会有助于英语世界的读者欣赏中国诗词的意美、音美和形美。

许渊冲

北京大学畅春园舞山楼

1992年12月26日

Translator's Note

• • •

Poetry should, said Mao Zedong, "be refined, regulated and rhymed." "New poetry should," said Lu Xun, "have rhythm and rhyme so that it might be easy for the reader to remember and recite." I think this is true not only of verse composition, but also of verse translation.

"The Chinese language," said Lu Xun, "is beautiful in three aspects: in sense so as to appeal to the heart, in sound so as to appeal to the ear and in form so as to appeal to the eye." In my opinion, translated verse should be as beautiful as the original in sense, in sound and in form.

"Poetry," wrote Mao Zedong to Chen Yi, "conceived in images, should not be so straightforward as prose." Images, I think, will show beauty in sense; regularity, beauty in form; and rhyme, beauty in sound.

"Prose," said Coleridge, "is words in the best order; poetry is the best words in the best order." The best words, in my opinion, are those beautiful in sense, sound and form.

As Mao's poems are beautiful not only in sense, but also in sound and in form, their translations should also be beautiful in these three aspects.

The basis of beauty lies in resemblance to the original. By resemblance we first mean the translation should be faithful to the original in sense, that is to say, there should be no mistranslation, nor should there be over- or under-translation. Compare the following versions of "On the Guangchang Road":

(1) O'erhead loom crags;
We go through the strong pass with wind-frozen red flags.

(2) Wind flutters the red flag as we march through the strong pass. (Tr. 1963)

(3) The wind unfurls the red flags,
As they climb over the mountain pass. (Tr. 1965)

(4) As we climb the pass
the wind plays open our red banners. (Tr. March 1972)

(5) Red flags, whirled by the wind,
go through the great pass. (Tr. August 1972)

(6) We cross the great pass, red flags waving in the wind. (Tr. 1976)

(7) And, red flags flapping in the wind,
Through the great pass we go. (Tr. 1978)

(8) We press ahead through the great pass,
The whirlwind flopping the red flags. (Tr. 1980)

The first version which describes the Red Army marching in snow with red flags frozen in the wind shows through what hardship and with what courage the soldiers were fighting, while the other versions which give pictures of red flags floating or flying in the wind by using "flutter, unfurl, play open, whirl, wave, flap, flop" are mistranslations.

As to translations overdone or underdone, we may read the following versions:

(1) The wind unrolls/Red flags like scrolls. ("New Year's Day")

(2) Red flags stream in the wind in a blaze of glory. (ibid.)

(3) How thick with salient days those bygone times appear! ("Changsha")

(4) Vivid yet those crowded months and years. (ibid.)

If the first and third versions are faithful to the original, then the second is overdone and the fourth underdone. The over- or under-translation does not resemble the orginal in sense, so it cannnot be so beautiful as the original.

Generally speaking, a faithful translation can more or less bring out the original beauty, for example,

(1) Waving my hand, I part from you. ("To Yang Kaihui")

But sometimes there is contradiction between resemblance and beauty, that is to say, a faithful translation may not bring out the beauty of the original, for instance,

(2) But in man's world seas change into mulberry fields.

(3) The world goes on with changes in the fields and oceans.

Version 2 is faithful, but it tells us only the particular fact that seas change into mulberry fields while Version 3 tells us the general truth that there will be changes in the fields and oceans, so the former is not so beautiful as the latter.

Beauty in sense may come from historical associations, then it will be lost in translation, but the loss can be made up for by poetic diction. For instance, we find in Shakespeare's *Macbeth* the following verse:

(1) New sorrows strike heaven on the face.

In translating "Against the First 'Encirclement' Campaign" we may use the verb as follows:

(2) The wrath of godlike warriors strikes the sky overhead.

For another example, we find in Shakespeare's *Othello* the following:

(3) The chidden billow seems to pelt the clouds.

The verb "to pelt" may be borrowed in translating "The Seaside":

(4) The clouds are pelted by breakers white.

Not only words but also phrases may be borrowed. For instance, in Shelley's "Ode to the West Wind" and "To a Skylark" we find the following:

(5) O wild West Wind, thou breath of Autumn's being,

(6) In the golden lightning
Of the sunken sun

We may use these phrases in translating "The Pass of Mount Lou":

(7) What wild west wind!

(8) The mountains are sea-blue,

The sunken sun blood-red.

Sometimes, even a whole clause may be imitated, for example, Byron wrote:

(9) When we two parted
In silence and tears

These two lines may be imitated in translating "Ode to the Mume Blossom":

(10) Then spring depart'd in wind and rain ...

Beauty in sense which may be associated with beauty in sound or in form will also be lost in translation, then we should choose the best possible poetic diction to make up for the loss. Let us compare two versions of one verse in "Ode to the Mume Blossom":

(1) When the mountain flowers are in full bloom

(2) When with blooming flowers the mountain is aflame

The original is not only beautiful in sense but also in sound. The "full bloom" in the first version is not so picturesque as "aflame" in the second; it has not made up for the loss in sound by using such alliterations as "flowers" and "flame." Read the following couplet in "The Long March":

(3) The five serpentine Ridges outspread like rippling rills;
The pompous Wumeng peaks tower but like mole-hills.

"serpentine" is not only faithful but also beautiful, as picturesque as the original; "rippling rills" makes us see the shape of the Ridges and hear the ripples by the use of alliteration and assonance, that is to say, beauty in sense is brought out when associated with beauty in sound or form; "pompous" resembles the original not only in sense but also in sound; "mole-hills" is not so faithful as "mud pills" but it is far more beautiful in sense and in sound and better matched with "rills."

To sum up, in order to bring out beauty in sense, we may choose the best possible words in the best possible order, borrow poetic diction from English and American poets and enhance beauty in sense by adding beauty in sound or in form so as to make up for the loss in either or both.

Beauty in sound lies chiefly in rhythm and rhyme. In Chinese poetry, rhythm consists chiefly in even and oblique tones, which may be represented by strong and weak beats in translation, that is to say, a verse may be translated in iambics, trochaics, anapaestics or dactylics. Classical Chinese poetry consists chiefly of five-character and seven-character lines. The former may be replaced by heroic couplets and the latter by Alexandrines.

As to rhymes, it would be a happy translation if the English rhymes could more or less resemble the Chinese. For instance, the first stanza of "The Warlords Fight" reads as follows:

(1) A sudden veer of wind and <u>rain</u>:
The warlords fight <u>again</u>.
Sowing on earth but grief and <u>pain</u>,
The dream of reigning but in <u>vain</u>.

The English rhymes read more or less like the original "bian, zhan, yuan, xian." For another example, the last three lines of

"Against the First 'Encirclement' Campaign" read as follows:

(2) Arouse a million workers and peasants to take the gun,
United as one,
How wild below Mount Pillar our red flags will run!

Not only the English vowels but also the English consonants resemble more or less the Chinese rhymes "gan, wan, luan." Read the following couplet in "Huichang":

(3) Our warriors, pointing south, see Guangdong loom
In a richer green and a lusher gloom.

The original beauty in sound is brought out by the use of rhymes, alliterations and assonances.

The first two examples show on what rare occasions English words may resemble Chinese characters in sound. In most cases, the English and the Chinese words are quite different. Therefore, it is not required to translate a Chinese character by a similar English word, but it is advisable to bring out the original beauty in sound. This is particularly difficult when the original is rich in repetition of characters. For example, we may compare two different versions of the first stanza of "Yellow Crane Tower":

(1) Wide, wide flow the nine streams through the land,
Dark, dark threads the line from south to north.
Blurred in the thick haze of the misty rain
Tortoise and Snake hold the great river locked.

(2) Nine wide, wide rivers over the heartland outspread;
One long, long railroad links north and south like a thread.

Shrouded in grizzling mist and drizzling rain,
Tortoise and Snake Hills hold the great river in chains.

In both versions, the repetition of characters in the first couplet is replaced by that of such words as "wide," "dark" or "long," while the repetition in the second couplet is replaced by "grizzling" and "drizzling" in the second version, which is far more picturesque than the first. The repetition may also be represented by the use of rhymes, alliterations and assonances, for instance,

(1) The boundless land is clad in white;
The endless waves are lost to sight. ("Snow")

(2) The misunderstanding arose from what I wrote,
But it will melt like clouds that fleet and mists that float. ("To Yang Kaihui")

Rhymes are used in the first version and alliterations in the second. Sometimes the repetition of characters is seperated in one verse, then it requires more artistic skill to represent it in translation. Compare the two versions of "Militia Women":

(1) How bright and brave they look, shouldering five-foot rifles
On the parade ground lit up by the first gleams of day.
China's daughters have high-aspiring minds,
The love their battle array, not silks and satins.

(2) So bright and brave, with rifles five feet long,
At early dawn they shine on drilling place.
Most Chinese daughters have a desire strong

To face the powder, not powder the face.

In the first version, alliteration is used to show the repetition of characters; in the second, "face" and "powder" are ingeniously repeated so as to bring out beauty in sense and in sound. In the first line of the original, alliteration is used, so in both versions "bright and brave" replace the original alliteration.

To sum up, we may use English metres to represent Chinese tones, English rhymes to replace Chinese rhymes, and alliterations, assonances and repetitions to bring out the original beauty in sound.

Beauty in form lies chiefly in line length and parallelism. If an English version could resemble the original in form, so much the better. For example, in translating a poem of sixteen characters, it would be better to represent one character by one English word as follows:

Peaks
Piercing the blue without blunting the blade,
The sky would fall
But for this colonnade.

The original consists of four lines of one, seven, three, five characters respectively. If the last word of the third line in this version is removed to the last line, then this version would resemble the original in form. But it is as difficult to resemble in form as in sound, so we should be contented to represent one Chinese character by one or two English words. For instance, there are four short lines of three characters in "The River All Red"; I think it would be good enough to translate them as follows:

(1) So many deeds
Bear no delay.
Sun and earth turn;
Time flies away.

(2) So many things
Should soon be done.
Sun and earth turn,
Time waits for none.

(3) With so much to do,
We must e'er make haste.
As sun and earth turn,
There's no time to waste.

(4) Many deeds should soon be done
At the earliest date.
The earth turns round the sun;
For no man will time wait.

Chinese poetry is full of parallelism. Generally speaking, the second and the third couplet of an ottava rima should be parallel. Parallelism is not only used in regulated poems but also in lyrics. In the example mentioned above,

The boundless land is clad in white;
The endless waves are lost to sight.

we find the adjective "boundless" parallel to "endless," the noun "land" balanced with "waves," the verb "is clad" paired with "are lost," and the phrase "in white" matched with "to sight." For another example, we may compare the two versions of the second couplet of "Winter Clouds":

(1) Chill waves sweep through steep skies,
Yet earth's gentle breath grows warm.

(2) In the steep sky cold waves are swiftly sweeping by;
On the vast earth warm winds gradually growing high.

In the first version there is no parallelism, but in the second, the subjects, verbs, adverbs and adverbial phrases in these two lines are well balanced. What is more, alliterations such as "swiftly sweeping" and "gradually growing" are used to represent the original repetition of characters so that beauty in sense, in sound and in form are all brought out.

As it is difficult to bring out the three beauties at once, it would be advisable to diminish the difficulty by preserving beauty in sound of one line and beauty in form of another. For instance, we may read the second stanza of "Get Away, Pest!":

The vernal wind awakens myriads of willows;
Six hundred million are masters of wisest sort.
Crimson rain, as we wish, turns into fertile billows;
Green mountains, if we will, to bridges give support.
Our iron arms remoulding three streams rock the land;
Our silver mattocks felling five peaks rend the sky.
Where will the God of Plague take flight? Burn tapers and
Paper boats to throw light upon his way on high!

"Billows" in line 3 rhymes with "willows" in line 1; "support" in line 4 rhymes with "sort" in line 2; "land" in line 5 rhymes with "and" in line 7 and "sky" in line 6 rhymes with "high" in line

8. Thus the difficulty in rhyming is shared by the first and last couplets, so we may concentrate our attention on parallelism in the second and third couplets.

To sum up, we should pay attention to line length and parallelism to bring out beauty in form. But beauty in form is not so important as beauty in sound, still less than beauty in sense; in other words, beauty in sense is of first-rate importance, beauty in sound of second-rate and beauty in form of third-rate. We should do our best to make our version as beautiful as the original in these three aspects. If it is impossible, we may first leave out resemblance in form as in sound, but we should try our possible to preserve the original beauty in sense and in sound.

If two English words can equally bring out the original beauty in sense, then we may choose the one more beautiful in sound. For example, in the above-mentioned verse,

The wind unrolls
Red flags like scrolls.

Both "unrolls" and "unfurls" can bring out the original beauty in sense, but "unrolls" can rhyme with "scrolls" and is more beautiful in sound; therefore, "unrolls" is the preferable word. Even if "unfurls" is more faithful to the original than "unrolls," say the former is 90% faithful and the latter 80%, still I would prefer "unrolls" for it is 80% beautiful while "unfurls" is only 50%. The score of the former is higher than that of the latter. In a word, the version which achieves the highest score is the best version.

Mao Zedong's poems have been translated into various foreign languages. So far as I know, there are at least eleven English editions:

1. *Nineteen Poems by Mao Tse-tung* translated by Andrew Boyd and published by Foreign Languages Press, Beijing, in 1958;

2. "Thirty-seven Poems by Mao Tse-tung" translated by Jerome Ch'en and Michael Bullock and included in *Mao and the Chinese Revolution* published by Oxford University Press, London, in 1965;

3. *Poems by Mao Tse-tung* translated by Dr. Wong Man and published by Eastern Horizon Press, Hong Kong, in 1966;

4. *Poems of Mao Tse-tung* translated by Hua-ling Nieh Engle and Paul Engle and published by Dell Publishing Co., New York, in 1972;

5. *The Poems of Mao Tse-tung* translated by Willis Barnstone and published by Harper & Row, New York, in 1972;

6. Mao Tse-tung's *Poems* published by Foreign Languages Press, Beijing, in 1976;

7. Mao Tse-tung's *Thirty-nine Poems* published by Nanjing University, Nanjing, in 1978;

8. *42 Poems of Mao Tse-tung* published by Luoyang Institute of Foreign Languages, Luoyang, in 1978;

9. *Mao Zedong's Poems* published by Hunan People's Publishing House, Changsha, in 1980;

10. *Reverberations—Poems of Mao Tse-tung* translated

by Nancy T. Lin and published by Joint Publishing Co., Hong Kong, in 1980;

11. *Earth-Shaking Songs—Epic of Chinese Revolution* including 43 poems of Mao Zedong translated by Xu Yuan-zhong and published by the Commercial Press Ltd., Hong Kong, in 1981.

"It is proper," said the Engles in the introduction to their version, "that the ruler of the country with the most people in the world should sell more copies of his book than any poet in history. It is probably true that the fifty-seven million copies said to have been sold of the poems of Mao Tse-tung may well equal the number of all volumes of poetry by all poets writing in English from the beginning of time." From this we can see the wide-spread influence of Mao Zedong's poetry in China and in the world. In 1986 a new selection of his poems was published in Beijing, including fifty poems in all. As his centennial anniversary falls in 1993, China Translation & Publishing Corporation agrees on the translation and publication of these fifty poems in commemoration of his great contribution to China and to the world. As Robert Payne said in his *White Pony*, "we can understand a people best through their poetry, and the Chinese who have written poetry since the beginning of time have always regarded poetry as the finest flower of their culture." So I think the publication of this new edition will bring about a better understanding in the English world of this great man and of Chinese culture from which he received a large inheritance and to which he made a great contribution.

"It is impossible," said the *Columbia Book of Chinese Poetry*, "to imagine poetry in English in our century without the influence and in some sense the presence of Chinese poetry." "At the present time," said Burton Watson, "some translators of Chinese poetry into English continue to press in the direction of even greater freedom, while others experiment in the reintroduction of rhyme and other formal elements that were earlier jettisoned. My own belief is that all types of innovation and experiment are to be welcomed, for from them hopefully will evolve even more effective methods for bringing the beauties of Chinese poetry over into English." I hope the publication of this present book will help the English readers to appreciate the beauty of Chinese poetry in sense, in sound and in form.

X.Y.Z.

Peking University

December 26, 1992

图书在版编目（CIP）数据

许渊冲英译毛泽东诗词：汉英对照 / 许渊冲编译. — 北京：中译出版社，2020.5（2024.2重印）

ISBN 978-7-5001-6058-8

Ⅰ. ①许… Ⅱ. ①许… Ⅲ. ①英语—汉语—对照读物 ②毛主席诗词 Ⅳ. ①H319. 4：A

中国版本图书馆CIP数据核字（2020）第036220号

出版发行　中译出版社
地　　址　北京市西城区新街口外大街28号普天德胜主楼4层
电　　话　(010) 68359827，68359303（发行部）；68359725（编辑部）
邮　　编　100044
传　　真　(010) 68357870
电子邮箱　book@ctph.com.cn
网　　址　http://www.ctph.com.cn

出 版 人　张高里
总 策 划　贾兵伟
策划编辑　胡晓凯
责任编辑　范祥镇

艺术顾问　费滨海
装帧设计　黄　浩
排　　版　北京竹页文化传媒有限公司
印　　刷　北京顶佳世纪印刷有限公司
经　　销　新华书店

规　　格　880 mm × 1230 mm　1/32
印　　张　9
插　　页　0.25
字　　数　100千字
版　　次　2020年5月第一版
印　　次　2024年2月第四次

ISBN 978-7-5001-6058-8　　　　定价：98.00元